ST. JOHN THE EVANGELIST CHURCH

WARRENTON, VIRGINIA
140 YEARS

December 1, 2001

Dear Parishioners,

    The Hunt Country of Fauquier County, Virginia, has many mileposts. Our 140 years is a special milestone for Catholicism here in Warrenton. Bishop McGill's first Mass at the home of Mr. and Mrs. Rice Payne in December of 1855 started the journey for St. John's Parish. The cornerstone was laid on July 16, 1860, and the humble red brick structure was dedicated on October 21, 1861. The parish outgrew the first church and moved into the second one on May 30, 1965.

    The church however, is not merely stone and mortar; it is people. The rich legacy given us by the founders of this parish is our challenge on the road of life here at St. John's. We, the Eucharistic Community of St. John the Evangelist Catholic Church, gather to celebrate our communion with God the Father, Christ the Teacher, and with the inspiration of the Holy Spirit, through worship, education, and community activities.

    In our life's journey, we endeavor to share our experience of Christ's love and mercy and to extend that experience to all sectors of the community through social concerns. In so doing, we form a haven where all are welcomed, all are challenged to proclaim and live the Gospel, and all are loved.

Your servant in Christ,

Rev. Michael J. Bazan,
Pastor

Walking

in Faith:

the first 25 Years

A History
of the
Diocese of Arlington

WITHDRAWN

By Anthony D. Andreassi

Table of Contents

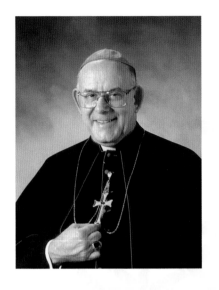

Dear Sisters and Brothers in Christ,

I am both privileged and proud to introduce this historical record of the first twenty-five years of our diocesan Church of Arlington.

We recall the lives and accomplishments of those who have formed and built up this diocesan church with grateful hearts. Their faith-filled vision and zealous labors have handed on to us a heritage that is rich in its two-fold love of God and neighbor. These forerunners of ours saw clearly the growth that was beginning to be visible, and throughout these twenty-five years, they responded with fidelity, generosity and sacrifice.

As benefactors of this legacy of faith, we seek to live the present with enthusiastic hearts. Energized by the clear examples of faith, hope and love recorded in this history, we now embrace the perennial mission of the Church first announced by the Lord Jesus and recently echoed by our Holy Father at the end of the Year of the Great Jubilee: "put out into the deep" – "*Duc in altum*" (*Lk 5: 4*).

We are so cognizant of the tremendous growth continuing to take place within the confines of this diocese! Authentic worship, formation in the faith, charitable outreach and persevering witness to the Truth: these engage our energies and efforts now and into the future. We must make Christ present through His Word and Sacraments, in His Body the Church and by our faithful witness. We must proclaim more by our lives than by our words the Gospel of love, of hope and of life.

Inspired by those whose testimonies of faith and deeds of love are recorded here, we look forward to the future with confident hearts. "Jesus Christ is the same yesterday, today and forever" (*Heb 13: 8*) – He goes before us even as He journeys with us. His promise remains: "Know that I am with you always, until the end of the world" (*Mt 28: 20*).

In this history of our first twenty-five years, we discover anew that witness of solid faith which encourages us to embrace the present with gospel love and to walk into our future with unwavering hope. Keeping before us the witness of these diocesan ancestors and strengthened by the prayerful intercession of Mary Immaculate and of our diocesan patrons, Saint Thomas More and Saint Elizabeth Ann Seton, we move ahead, together weaving the continuation of our diocesan history. "The Risen Jesus accompanies us on our way and enables us to recognize him, as the disciples of Emmaus did, 'in the breaking of the bread' (*Lk 24: 35*). May he find us watchful, ready to recognize his face and run to our brothers and sisters with the good news: 'We have seen the Lord' (*Jn 20: 25*)" (*Tertio Millennio Ineunte*, no. 59).

Faithfully in Christ,

+Paul S. Loverde

Most Reverend Paul S. Loverde
Bishop of Arlington

Preface

The United States Capitol may dominate its surroundings and stand as a powerful symbol of the nation, yet its shadow, even in late evening, does not reach beyond the famous Hill to which it lends its name. The same cannot be said of the capital city. During the course of the last century, the District of Columbia has become a gigantic magnet drawing people from all over the land to fill new offices required by the expansion of the nation after World War II. The effect has been a dramatic spillover of population into Northern Virginia. And because during the same period immigrant Catholics joined the mainstream, the development of the Catholic Church in the area has both affected and benefited from the expanding universe of Washington, DC.

The First Catholics in Virginia

Introduction

*F*or most people in Northern Virginia and the suburbs of Washington, D.C., Tuesday, August 13, 1974, was just another workday with typical hot and humid mid-summer weather. However, the atmosphere across the Potomac River in the nation's capital was anything but normal. Five days earlier, Richard M. Nixon had become the first American president to resign from office. Although "our long national nightmare was over," few Americans were in a joyful mood. For reasons having little to do with politics, the Catholic community of Northern Virginia was celebrating new beginnings, for on that day the "Diocese of Arlington" was officially born.

Earlier that year, on May 28, Pope Paul VI had announced the establishment of this new diocese in the Commonwealth of Virginia. Before this, the Diocese of Richmond had comprised the entire state of Virginia (and eight counties in West Virginia).

The Diocese of Arlington in Northern Virginia includes twenty-one counties: Arlington, Clarke, Culpeper, Fairfax, Fauquier, Frederick, King George, Lancaster, Loudoun, Madison, Northumberland, Orange, Page, Prince William, Rappahannock, Richmond, Shenandoah, Spotsylvania, Stafford, Warren and Westmoreland and seven independent cities: Alexandria, Fairfax, Falls Church, Fredericksburg, Manassas, Manassas Park and Winchester.

With this new foundation, the Bishop of Arlington would shepherd the Catholics living in twenty-one counties and seven cities of Northern Virginia. The new 6,541 square-mile see would be bordered by the Potomac River on the north and east, West Virginia on the west, and the far reaches of Shenandoah, Page, Madison, Orange, and Spotsylvania counties along the Rappahannock River on the south. Bishop Walter Sullivan of Richmond had asked the Holy Father to create a new diocese in that part of Virginia. A few years earlier Bishop John Russell, Sullivan's predecessor, had commissioned a committee of clergy and laity to look into the advisability of such a change. After their study, the committee recommended the division.

In petitioning the pope to establish a separate diocese for Northern Virginia, church leaders largely based their request on the region's recent growth, which was predicted to continue. Like the nation as a whole, the area was feeling the effects of the post-World War II baby boom as well as the increase in population

George Town

POTOMAC RIVER

EASTERN BRANCH

Lat. Capitol 38: 53, N.
Long. _____ 0: 0.

The District of Columbia was created by an act of Congress in 1789. As the size of federal bureaucracy expanded in the twentieth century, Washington's suburbs in Maryland and Virginia also experienced substantial growth. It was this development that led to the creation of the Diocese of Arlington in 1974.

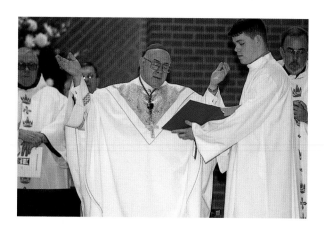

While many American dioceses have been forced to close churches in recent years, the Diocese of Arlington has had difficulty building large enough churches to accommodate the growing number of Catholics attending Mass in many of the diocese's parishes. On February 27, 2001, Bishop Paul Loverde, the third Bishop of Arlington, celebrated a Mass dedicating a new, larger church for Christ the Redeemer Parish, Sterling. Left to right: Father Daniel O'Shea, S.A., Bishop Paul Loverde, Robert Munroe, Father Arthur M. Johnson, S.A.

that came as a result of a greatly expanded federal government. In 1974, the total population of the area that was to become the Arlington diocese was about 1.2 million, while an estimate for the year 2000 put the population at over 2.3 million. The growth of the Catholic population has been even more dramatic. In 1974, Catholics numbered about 144,000. By 2001 that figure had more than doubled to 368,575. Such population expansion made establishment of a separate jurisdiction for the Catholic community of Northern Virginia not only feasible, but also necessary.

This division was not the first time Rome had split an American see to make a new one. In fact, the several dozen dioceses in the eastern third of the United States had come about by a series of divisions occurring throughout the nineteenth and twentieth centuries. Originally the entire region was part of the Diocese of Baltimore, which in 1789 had been made the first American see. However, the beginnings of the Catholic community in what is now the United States go back more than two hundred years before this.

Colonial Virginia

Although most of the seventeenth-century English immigrants who came to British

North America were Protestant, a few thousand English Catholics braved the Atlantic and struggled to make a home in the New World. Along with a scattering of their co-religionists from other European lands, they continued to practice a faith that in parts of the Old World had brought them scorn and disenfranchisement at a minimum, and sometimes even martyrdom. Though a few Catholics had settled in Virginia by the middle of the seventeenth century, they had originally come to Maryland, the birthplace of the American Catholic community. However, they were not the first Catholics to visit the region that was to become known as Virginia.

Almost forty years before the founding of Jamestown, a Spanish expedition set out from St. Augustine in 1570 to explore the Chesapeake region. With them came a few missionaries of the newly founded Society of Jesus. Led by Father Baptista de Segura, these missionaries were eventually separated from the main party. By 1572 the entire group had suffered

"Death of Father John Baptista de Segura, S.J., and His Companions." From Societas Militans (1675).

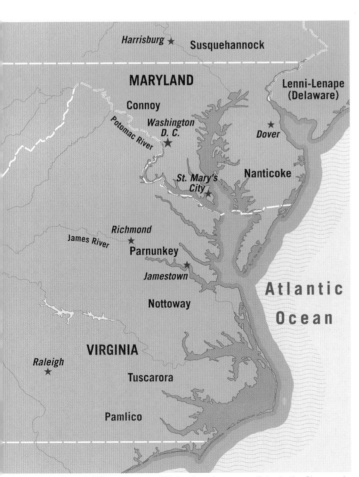

Several different groups of Native Americans were living in the Chesapeake region when the English colonists first arrived.

martyrdom near the future site of Jamestown. A Catholic presence did not return to Virginia for almost seventy years, but this time its provenance was not Spanish.

The violent persecution of Catholics had taken a temporary hiatus under King Charles I (r. 1625-1640), yet the harsh laws that prevented them from full participation in civic life remained. So, in 1634 Cecil Calvert, a member of the English Catholic gentry and the second Lord Baltimore, acted on a royal grant given to his father. He sponsored the foundation of the Maryland colony as a haven for Catholics (though from the beginning onward, Protestants were in the majority). Conscious of the magnanimity of King Charles in allowing such a venture, Calvert named the new colony for the king's Catholic wife, Henrietta Maria.

Soon after arriving, the Catholic colonists discovered that a small number of Catholic indentured servants were living in nearby Virginia. The Jesuits, joined by a few of the wealthier members of the community, quickly came to the aid of their co-religionists. Some of the gentry

St. James, Falls Church

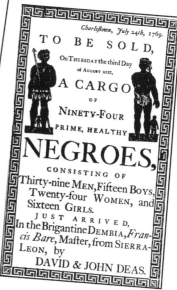

Above: A roadside marker on Route 1 in Aquia commemorates the first Catholic settlers in colonial Virginia. (Photo: Andres Martinez). Pamphlets boasting of the great opportunities that lay in store for settlers in North America made their way around England throughout the seventeenth century.
Right: In 1619 a Dutch man-of-war brought to Jamestown the first African slaves in the thirteen original colonies. Slave auctions were common in colonial and post-revolutionary times. In fact, until 1850 human beings were bought and sold within sight of the U.S. Capitol.

bought out the servants' contracts and brought them to Maryland where both groups were attempting to forge a better life than they had known in England. However, the honeymoon for Maryland Catholicism was short-lived. In the 1640s, Puritan radicals seized control of the Maryland government and initiated a wave of anti-Catholic violence. In response, a small group of Catholics, including a few Jesuits, took refuge across the Potomac in Virginia. When peace was restored, most returned home to Maryland. *However, a few Catholics decided to remain in Virginia.*

Around 1651 Giles Brent, a member of the colony's Catholic gentry and a former assistant governor of Maryland, fell into disfavor with the Calvert family and settled his family, including his Indian-princess wife, in Virginia. He staked out a homestead on the north

Aware that an exclusively Catholic colony would arouse the ire of English Protestants, Cecil Calvert, the second Lord Baltimore, was adamant that all Christian religions be tolerated in his Maryland colony.

side of the Aquia Creek on the Northern Neck of Virginia, the peninsula between the Rappahannock and Potomac Rivers in modern-day Stafford County. Giles Brent was soon joined by his two sisters, Margaret and Mary. Eventually the family was farming several plantations named "Peace," "Retirement" and "Harmony," covering more than eleven thousand acres. The family's land possessions continued to grow expanding as far north as present-day Alexandria. After Giles Brent's death, control of the family's property passed to his cousin, George Brent.

This other Brent was a successful lawyer, and despite his Catholic background, George Brent was respected by Virginia's Protestant ruling class because of his help in a colonial campaign against the Seneca Indians. *With the accession to the throne of King James II (r. 1685-88),*

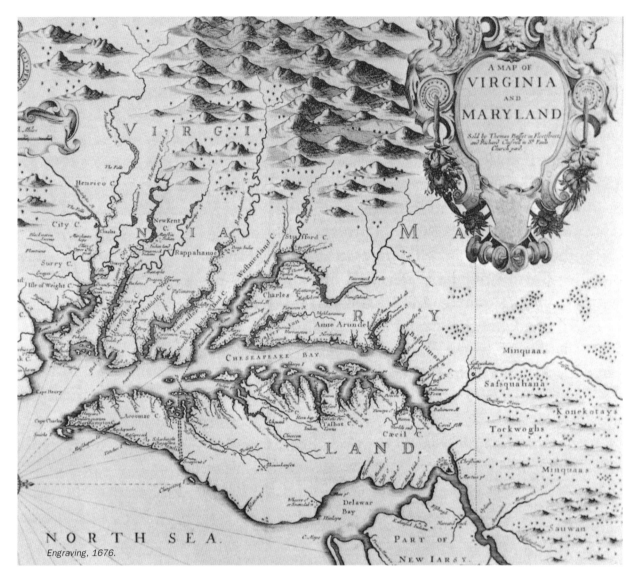

A MAP OF VIRGINIA AND MARYLAND

Engraving, 1676.

the last English Catholic monarch, George Brent was appointed Virginia's attorney general in 1686 and held a seat in the House of Burgesses, the only Catholic to do so in colonial Virginia. During his brief tenure as a public figure, George Brent gained further prominence because of his spirit of religious toleration in attempting to resettle a group of French Huguenots who had escaped to England fleeing persecution. (The Huguenots never came in the numbers expected, but thanks to Brent's work, a small group did settle in Virginia.) With the coronation of William and Mary in 1689 and the end of religious toleration for Catholics in Virginia and the rest of British North America, George Brent lost his governmental posts. He died in 1699.

Despite its small size, Roman authorities did not allow Virginia's Catholic community to go unnoticed. Acting more on the personal request of

Queen Henrietta Maria rather than on any real administrative need, Pope Urban VIII established the "Prefecture Apostolic of Virginia" (a sort of junior diocese) in 1650 and appointed Father Mantial, Capuchin Franciscan as the prefect (administrator). Because of the tiny number of Catholics and the re-enactment of harsh anti-Catholic laws after 1689, this prefecture quickly passed out of existence.

The Protestant ascendancy of 1689 brought an end to many of the advances made by Catholics in the colonies, yet Virginia's small Catholic community did not simply fade away. Rather, for the next hundred years their numbers held steady (probably fewer than one hundred) with the community centered on the Brent plantations. However, in the effort not to antagonize their Protestant neighbors, Virginia's Catholics practiced

The colonists and their leaders harbored a strong dislike and suspicion of Catholics. This fear intensified after a Puritan uprising in Maryland caused a number of Catholics from this neighboring colony to seek refuge in Virginia.

their faith in a private, unobtrusive way and very often without the regular ministrations of a priest. (They were not unlike Catholics back in England who during these times were once known as a "*gens lucifuga*" or a "people fleeing the light.") While several other colonial Catholic families became Protestant during the eighteenth century, most notably the Calverts, the Brents remained Catholic. *From 1690 to the time of the American Revolution, the Brents were the only known Catholic family in Virginia.*

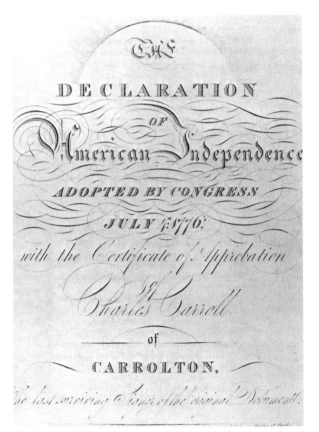

Charles Carroll of Carrollton, a cousin to Bishop John Carroll, was the only Catholic to sign the Declaration of Independence. Reputed to be the richest man in the colonies at the time of the American Revolution, he is also remembered as the longest-living signer of the document. Carroll died in 1832.

The Early Republic

In the years following the American Revolution, as a result of the influx of newly arrived, mostly Irish, immigrants to the port cities of Norfolk and Alexandria, Virginia's Catholic population experienced slow but steady growth. Evidence for this can be found in the writings of Father John Dubois, a French émigré priest who later became Bishop of New York. In a letter dated November 1791, Dubois, who was living in Richmond, offered to make regular visitations to the small Catholic community in Alexandria, which at this time was the only part of the future Arlington diocese with any sizable Catholic presence. Dubois was never called upon to live up to his offer since priests teaching at nearby Georgetown College came in on weekends to celebrate the sacraments. However, some of the laity were not satisfied with this half measure and began agitating for a full-time priest and a permanent house of worship.

The real father of the Catholic community in Alexandria was Colonel John Fitzgerald, an Irish-born Catholic, who served as one of George Washington's aides-de-camp during the Revolutionary War. On St. Patrick's Day 1788, Fitzgerald hosted a religiously diverse assemblage of the leading citizens of Maryland and Virginia (including Washington) at his home in Alexandria to discuss the advisability of building a Catholic church in this city. Though unfortunately a transcript of these historic discussions is not extant, the record does state that shortly after this meeting, Fitzgerald began laying plans for a permanent Catholic church in Alexandria. The work soon came to completion. In 1795 St. Mary's church was officially dedicated.

Fr. Francis Ignatius Neale, S.J., was pastor of St. Mary's Church, Alexandria, from 1795 to 1818.

John Carroll.

In keeping with the ecumenical spirit that marked the beginnings of St. Mary's, the parish's first church building was constructed on property that had been donated by a wealthy Protestant. (The original church structure no longer exists.) Since it was forbidden by law to build a Catholic church within the city of Alexandria, the site was chosen because it lay outside the city limits. *St. Mary's claims the unique distinction of being not only the first and oldest Catholic parish in the Diocese of Arlington, but also in the entire state of Virginia.*

It was in 1789, six years before the dedication of St. Mary's in Alexandria, that the first American diocese was created with Baltimore as its center. After its creation, Rome asked the priests of the United States to choose their new bishop. By a vote of twenty-six to two, they elected Father John Carroll, a native of Maryland and a distant relative of the Brents. Carroll had been serving as a vicar apostolic, or superior, for American Catholics, a role held by a cleric who has much of the administrative power of a bishop, but who lacks episcopal ordination.

With Carroll's consecration and nomination as Bishop of Baltimore, the Church in Virginia, still limited principally to Alexandria, Norfolk and Richmond, became part of a regular diocese, just as local churches in Europe had been administered for centuries.

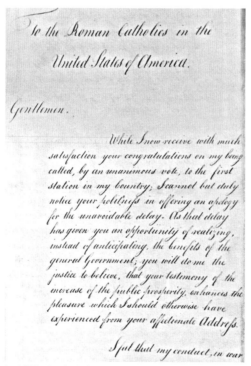

In 1789 the Catholic community sent a joint letter of congratulations to newly elected President Washington. Unlike others of his time, Washington seemed to harbor no antipathy for Catholics. In fact, during the Revolution, he commanded his troops not to engage in the traditional anti-Catholic rituals on Guy Fawkes Day (November 5) so as not to antagonize French Catholics in Quebec whose support the Revolutionaries were courting.

Virginia Gets Its Own Diocese

*D*uring the first two decades of the nineteenth century, the Catholic Church in the United States grew at a slow but steady pace. *At the end of the American Revolution, then-Father Carroll estimated Catholics to number about one per cent of the general population, with the largest concentration in Maryland and Pennsylvania.*

In 1808 New York, along with Boston, Philadelphia and Bardstown, had been made into separate dioceses. By the 1820s this number had grown to almost 200,000.

In 1820 Rome made new dioceses in Richmond, Virginia, and Charleston, South Carolina. However, unlike the divisions made in 1808, the new sees had not been created mainly to satisfy the needs of the growing Catholic communities. Instead, Rome was attempting to bring an end to a quarrel between Archbishop Ambrose Marechal of Baltimore and the lay trustees in South Carolina and Virginia who held the legal deeds to

The Diocese of Baltimore (c. 1804) included all of the United States.

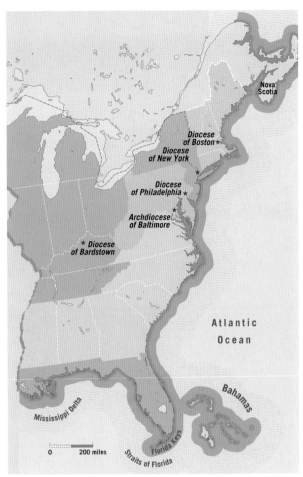

The American Catholic Church in 1808.

church property. The trustees argued that a pastor and his bishop had only spiritual authority over the parish while trustees were responsible for the temporal concerns of the church. Marechal and other American bishops engaged in the debate were the ultimate victors. In this particular battle, the trustees won the day in gaining separation from Baltimore and Marechal's authority.

The Roman authorities were quick to locate the cathedral in Charleston for the new diocese in South Carolina. However, they were more hesitant in regard to the site for Virginia's cathedral.

In the discussion, one official suggested Hartford (Connecticut) as a suitable spot!

Bishop Patrick Kelly, first Bishop of Richmond (1820-22).

He could only be disabused of this proposal after being shown a map. Eventually, Richmond was chosen as the episcopal seat.

The new Richmond diocese included all of Virginia and what later became West Virginia, but not the city of Alexandria, which until 1846, remained a part of the District of Columbia and under the jurisdiction of the Archbishop of Baltimore. Patrick Kelly, a native of Ireland, was named the first bishop, but, in fact, never made it to Richmond. After his consecration, he lingered in Norfolk where he taught school to support himself. But in June 1822, he left Virginia for Ireland to shepherd greener pastures as Bishop of Waterford and Lismore.

Baptism of the Lord (St. John, McLean)

After arriving in Ireland, Kelly sent a report to Rome detailing the status of his previous diocese. *In a total population, which he estimated at about one million, he reckoned the Catholic community to number about 1,200 centered mostly in Norfolk, Richmond and Martinsburg.* This far-flung congregation was served by only five priests. Virginia's Catholics would have to wait twenty years before Rome would appoint a successor to Kelly.

The Need for Priests

Father Richard Vincent Whelan, a priest working in Martinsburg and its environs, was named the second Bishop of Richmond in 1841. *In his pastoral letter, Whelan lamented that Catholicism had a stronger presence on the "prairies of the distant West" than in Virginia where "the very name [Catholic] is scarcely known."* To change this, Whelan planned to actively recruit Catholic families and priests for his new diocese. He immediately set to work to build a seminary.

True to his convictions, Whelan did open and operate a seminary; however, it lasted just five years and produced only four priests. Like other bishops of clergy-poor dioceses, Whelan turned to Ireland for help. In 1842 the Congregation of the Mission, a Vincentian community, had opened All Hallows Missionary College just outside Dublin to train priests for the foreign missions. (All Hallows ordained over 10,000 priests and sent them to serve in places all over the English-speaking world, from Northern Virginia to western Australia.) In his letter to the seminary rector, Whelan described the life for which a future

Bishop Richard V. Whelan, second Bishop of Richmond (1841-1851).

Virginia priest must gird himself:

[The man] must expect a life of great labour & fatigue, much exposure to cold, heat & rain, bad roads, very indifferent diet & lodging, but little respect for his dignity, few Catholics, little of society, a compensation barely adequate to support himself in the plainest & most economical manner... I want no priest who does not come fully prepared to enter upon such a charge... make the young men whom you may think of selecting fully aware of this, inform them that there are places much more desirable elsewhere, where they may labor more advantageously, & that if they select my diocese I shall regard their character & honor compromised if afterwards they flinch, & I shall refuse an exeat [permission to leave] where there is no other good and controlling motive.

A modern Pieta. (St. Mark, Vienna)

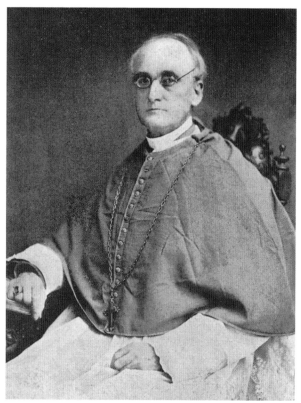

Bishop John McGill, third Bishop of Richmond (1851-1872).

until his death in 1872. It fell to McGill to see the Richmond diocese through the Civil War.

Civil War and Reconstruction

*A*t the outbreak of war in 1861, Northern Virginia had only three churches to serve all its Catholics, and two of them had been opened in just the previous three years. In 1858 Father Peter Kroes, the Jesuit pastor of St. Mary's in Alexandria, constructed a

Mary and the Beloved Disciple at the foot of the cross. (St. Catherine of Siena, Great Falls)

Such is not like the fare found in present-day priestly vocation brochures. However, Whelan was honest and wanted any future Virginia priest to know what he would be getting himself into. Despite the diocese's gloomy description, seven Irish seminarians signed up to serve as priests of the Richmond diocese, and these men were only the beginning. *Over the last century and a half, Virginia has become home to more missionary priests from All Hallows than any other state except California.* When these Irish priests began arriving, they soon realized that a growing number of their fellow countrymen were also making a new home in Virginia. By the middle of the nineteenth century, a large number of Irishmen had come to the state to work on the rapidly expanding system of railroads and canals, two infrastructure projects that were largely responsible for the increase in the Catholic population of Virginia.

In 1851 Whelan's tenure as Bishop of Richmond came to an end when he was transferred to the newly established Diocese of Wheeling, which was to cover the northwestern part of Virginia. He was succeeded by Father John McGill of Louisville, Kentucky, who remained Bishop of Richmond

mission church in Fairfax Station and placed it under the patronage of "Our Lady of the Snows." Also in that year, another church with the name of St. Mary's was established in Fredericksburg. The growth in the Catholic community in both these areas came as a result of the influx of Irish laborers who had come to work on the railroad. Any

Opposite: For more than a century the Catholics in Virginia and many other parts of the U.S. had to rely on priests from Ireland to supplement the less than adequate supply of native-born clergy. These Irish missionaries left their mark on American Catholicism in many ways, especially through their devotion to St. Patrick, who is co-patron of Ireland, along with St. Brigid.

St. Patrick, Fredericksburg

thought of building other churches was laid to rest with the coming of war.

Since Richmond served as the capital of the Confederacy for much of the Civil War, it is not surprising that Bishop McGill championed the Southern cause, and on several occasions he made public displays of his support. For example, after hostilities had commenced, he ordered priests to discontinue praying for the United States during Mass, but to support the Confederate authorities in their intentions instead. He even contemplated prohibiting Union chaplains from hearing confessions in Virginia.

With episcopal support, Virginia's Catholic men took up arms to defend the slavery and the "aggression" of the North. Several hundred Catholics enthusiastically donned the gray uniform, and some even banned together to form separate Irish-Catholic regiments.

Catholic women in Virginia also played an important role during the Civil War. Several hundred religious sisters served as nurses in army hospitals and camps during the bloody conflict. *In Virginia several dozen Daughters of Charity ministered to the wounded, regardless of the soldier's faith or the color of his uniform.* The sisters took in hundreds of wounded into their hospitals in Portsmouth and Richmond and were even given charge of a few military hospitals. Despite their great display of generosity, the dedication of the sisters could not entirely put to rest the anti-Catholic sentiment that had been a part of Virginia since its beginnings. For example, a soldier recuperating in a hospital operated by sisters was asked if he wanted to become a Catholic. He quickly replied "No," adding that he did not care for Catholicism, though he admitted that he had never met a Catholic. However, he said that he might consider joining the "sisters' church." Although this particular soldier did not become a Catholic, there

In 1937, Father Clarence J. Howard, who was black, and a native of Norfolk, Virginia was ordained a priest making him at that time one of eight African-American priests in the U.S. and one of only twelve in all of the Americas. At that time most religious orders and many seminaries in the U.S. would not admit black candidates. This policy began to change after the Second World War.

are several recorded instances of Protestant soldiers who decided to convert, thanks to the good example of these women religious.

Although the Confederate cause eventually succumbed to defeat, like most other Southerners, Virginia's Catholics were relieved to have peace once again. Despite the huge number of dead and the disruption and destruction, the war had left in its wake, most Southern whites resumed life as it was before the war. As for most of the newly emancipated African Americans, their lives changed very little. Southern blacks would have to wait until the Civil Rights Movement in the 1950s and 60s before real improvement would come to their lives.

As Whelan had done before him, Bishop McGill began recruiting priests, this time at the American College in Louvain. Since so few of the newly emancipated African Americans were Catholic, McGill saw the potential for a great harvest for priests with apostolic zeal. However, he was honest enough to admit that there could be little hope for a great influx of new black Catholics, given the few priests and limited resources at his disposal. *In Virginia as in the rest of the South, where the overwhelming number of African Americans still resided, relatively few were converted to Roman Catholicism in the decades after emancipation. In fact, even today only about one percent of blacks are Catholic.*

After the death of McGill in 1872, Bishop James Gibbons of Baltimore was appointed fourth Bishop of Richmond and continued in his role as vicar apostolic of North Carolina to which he had been appointed in 1868. Gibbons' time in Virginia would be brief, for higher offices lay in his future. Until

Before becoming Archbishop of Baltimore, James Cardinal Gibbons served as the fourth Bishop of Richmond (1872-1878).

Bishop John J. Keane, fifth Bishop of Richmond (1878-1888).

his departure for Baltimore, Gibbons had responsibility for the spiritual welfare of about 17,000 Catholics living in a 34,800 square-mile territory. He quickly threw himself into his work.

Compared to bishops in urban dioceses who were building new churches at breakneck speed, the bishops of Richmond were slow in erecting new parishes in their jurisdictions. However, three new parishes were founded in Northern Virginia in addition to the churches in Alexandria, Fredericksburg and Fairfax Station. In 1870 Sacred Heart in Winchester was raised from the status of a mission to an independent parish. In 1873 St. James in Falls Church was built as another mission of Alexandria, and in 1874 St. John the Evangelist in Warrenton was begun.

Like McGill, Gibbons wanted to begin an outreach to the African-American community and asked for missionaries from Herbert Vaughan, superior of English Mill Hill Fathers, a newly established missionary congregation headquartered in London.

Although Vaughan gave an indication that he would be willing to help, no Mill Hill priests ever

actually came. However, Gibbons remained undaunted and kept looking for help. Although he was never ultimately successful, later in the century, priests and brothers from the Society of St. Joseph (Josephites), an American offshoot of Mill Hill which was founded specifically to work with African and Native Americans, did come to Virginia, eventually working in Alexandria, Lynchburg and Norfolk.

During these final decades of the century, Virginia's Catholic population continued to grow slowly but steadily. Some Catholics took on a more prominent role in society. *In 1870 Anthony J. Keiley became the first Catholic mayor of Richmond.* James Dooley held a seat in the state legislature and John J. Johnston represented his state in the U.S. Senate for two terms.

With Gibbons' promotion to archbishop of Baltimore in 1878, John J. Keane, a priest of Baltimore, was appointed the fifth Bishop of Richmond. A native of Ireland, Keane had most recently served as a parish priest in Washington, D.C. While in Richmond, Keane put heart and soul into his pastoral work, but as in the past, the

Richmond diocese was to serve as a stepping stone for its ordinary, and Keane would spend only ten years there.

While he was bishop, Keane placed strong emphasis on the formation of his clergy, holding conferences for his priests to encourage both their spiritual as well as intellectual development. He also believed strongly in the need for a well articulated lay spirituality. To support his conviction, Keane arranged for the Paulists (a missionary order of priests founded in the United States) to conduct a series of parish missions throughout the diocese.

In 1888 Keane left Richmond to become the first rector (president) of the Catholic University of America, which had been founded four years earlier. He was succeeded by Augustine van de Vyver, a native of Belgium and priest of the Richmond diocese who served as bishop until his death in 1911. During his twenty-three years in Richmond, van de Vyver continued the work of his predecessors in building up the Church in Virginia. He too traveled to Europe to recruit priests and even ordained his nephew, who served at various churches in the state, including St. Mary's in Alexandria.

In the late 1960s St. Ambrose in Annandale held liturgies in a provisional church. Left to right: Deacon Ronald Ruth, Father John Rea and Father James Grealish.

It was during van de Vyver's time as bishop that the Church in Northern Virginia began to experience growth. At the end of the nineteenth century, with the construction of a canal bridge, the region along the Potomac was finally connected with Maryland and Washington. This brought increased commerce and growth in the population. However, rapid and sustained expansion would not come until the middle of the twentieth century.

A New Century Brings Growth

Apart from a few mission stations visited by circuit-riding priests, *by the end of the nineteenth century only six churches served all of Northern Virginia.* They included: St. Mary's in Alexandria, St. Mary's in Fairfax Station, St. Mary's in Fredericksburg, Sacred Heart of Jesus in Winchester, St. James in Falls Church and St. John the Evangelist in Warrenton. However, this would soon change. New growth to the region would compel Bishop van de Vyver and his

Bishop Augustine van de Vyver, sixth Bishop of Richmond (1888-1911).

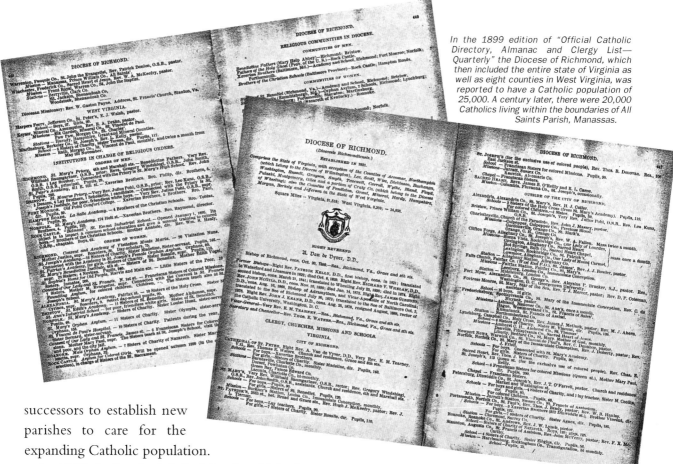

In the 1899 edition of "Official Catholic Directory, Almanac and Clergy List— Quarterly" the Diocese of Richmond, which then included the entire state of Virginia as well as eight counties in West Virginia, was reported to have a Catholic population of 25,000. A century later, there were 20,000 Catholics living within the boundaries of All Saints Parish, Manassas.

successors to establish new parishes to care for the expanding Catholic population.

In 1892 the Jesuits left St. Mary's, which they had staffed for almost a century. At the time of their departure, St. James in Falls Church (which had been a mission of Alexandria) was made a separate parish and Bishop van de Vyver named Father Edward Tearney as the first pastor. A few years later Tearney opened a parish school and brought in the Sisters of Perpetual Adoration to staff it. However, these sisters remained for only a short time. In 1923 the Servants of the Immaculate Heart of Mary (I.H.M.) came from Philadelphia to teach in the school. In the 1930's their ministry expanded and some I.H.M. sisters began traveling to Leesburg to teach religious education. In 1952 the sisters expanded their teaching ministry and opened an academy, which eventually relocated to a site near Lynchburg. However, in 1983 the school was closed because of declining enrollment.

St. Thomas à Becket, the patron of the parish in Reston, was martyred in the twelfth century for opposing the English king's attempt to assume powers traditionally held by the Church.

Much of the growth of Northern Virginia resulted from the introduction of trolley cars, which provided a cheap and quick method of transportation. The trolley's popularity spurred the region's development by allowing people to live farther away from their place of work, which at this time was centered mostly in Washington. In 1909 with the establishment of St. Charles Borromeo in the Clarendon section, Arlington received its first Catholic parish. Four years later Father Frederick Lackey, St. Charles' first pastor, began celebrating Mass in the Cherrydale section of Arlington for about one hundred parishioners. At first, the mission rented space in a grocery store and then a movie theater. In 1920 a church was built and placed under the patronage of St. Agnes. Shortly thereafter a permanent church was dedicated.

On October 8, 1915, ground was broken for St. Joseph Church in Alexandria, the first parish for blacks in Northern Virginia.

For much of the twentieth century the establishment of new parishes in Northern Virginia tended to follow the major transportation lines crossing the region since the expansion in population was clustered along these arteries. During the earlier decades, the new churches were founded along the rail lines because rail was still the region's main form of transportation. In 1919 a resident priest was assigned to the parish in Fairfax, located at the northern part of a railroad that ran south to Charlottesville. Using the rail to visit each of his stations, he soon began servicing a series of missions down the line. After the death of van de Vyver in 1911, Bishop Denis J. O'Connell was named his replacement. Born in Ireland, O'Connell was ordained for the Richmond diocese in 1877 and worked there for a few years before his career took him to Rome, Washington, D.C., and San Francisco. In 1911 O'Connell returned to his home diocese to become its seventh bishop. He would shepherd the Catholics of Virginia during the First World War and the development that the war

Mother Mary Lange

effort would bring to Northern Virginia. Even before the war, some parts of the region had seen growth. For example, the Catholic population of Alexandria had increased sufficiently by 1914 to warrant the establishment of St. Rita's as the city's second Catholic parish.

Although the United States did not enter the war until 1917, from early in the conflict, American industry increased production to supply materials to the Allies. This expansion in trade was a boon to the overall U.S. economy and to Northern Virginia in particular. With new business, Alexandria's shipyards soon hummed with activity that brought new workers to the city. This influx of laborers and their families, many of which remained after the war's end, brought about an increase in the city's Catholic population.

It had long been the desire of the American hierarchy that each parish should conduct an elementary school. In response to the growing number of children in his parish, the pastor of St. Mary's decided to open a school under the direction

Father Paul R. Cauwe, C.I.C.M., and the 1956 First Communion class of St. John's Parish, McLean.

Amleto G. Cardinal Cicognani, who served as apostolic delegate to the American hierarchy from 1933 to 1958, conveyed Pope Pius XII's blessings on the occasion of the sesquicentennial anniversary of the founding of St. Mary's in Alexandria.

of the Xaverian Brothers. It was not the first Catholic school in the city. The Sisters of the Holy Cross had already operated a parish-affiliated academy in Alexandria. However, the academy's tuition placed it beyond the reach of most working-class Catholic families. The new St. Mary's elementary school would be free and open to the children of all parishioners. The academy, which was later known as St. Mary's High School, closed in 1988.

During his fourteen years as Bishop of Richmond, O'Connell oversaw the slow but steady growth of the Catholic population of the diocese, thanks to improved transportation and a reinvigorated economy brought on by the First World War. The popularity and increasing affordability of the automobile were also responsible for the expansion of population in Northern Virginia. This was especially true after the construction of the Francis Scott Key Bridge in 1923 and the Arlington Memorial Bridge in 1932. Both attracted potential residents to Northern Virginia with the promise of an easy and quick commute. However, much of this expansion ground to a halt with the onset and deepening of the Great Depression in the Thirties. Strong growth would not return to the region until after the Second World War and the economic boom times of the 1950s.

In 1926 Andrew J. Brennan, Auxiliary Bishop of Scranton, took charge of the diocese. However, his influence in the diocese would be limited by a stroke he suffered in 1934. Before his illness Brennan launched a "Five-Year Plan" that called for the foundation of new parishes and the opening of more Catholic schools. His proposals for expansion were greatly inhibited by the Depression, and plans for new construction had to be put on hold for sunnier days.

Postwar Boom

Because of Brennan's physical incapacity, in 1935 Peter Leo Ireton was named coadjutor bishop and effectively ran the diocese for the next ten years until Brennan's formal resignation in

Holy Cross

One of only twelve Cistercian monasteries for men in the United States, Holy Cross Abbey in Berryville, Virginia, was founded after a devastating fire destroyed Our Lady of the Valley in Rhode Island in March, 1950. (The Cistercian Order goes back to late eleventh-century France and St. Robert of Molesme who set up the first Cistercian abbey as a renewal of Benedictine monasticism.) In November 1950, Dom Edmund Futterer, abbot of Our Lady of the Valley, sent 30 of his displaced monks to start a new foundation in the Shenandoah Valley of Northern Virginia. Before arriving, the monks had purchased some 1,200 acres and several buildings owned by the Wormeley family, and the monks immediately moved into the stone house, which dates to 1784. The community continues to inhabit this building, which over the years has been renovated and enlarged.

After steady growth, in 1958 a Cistercian General Chapter made Holy Cross an independent abbey and Father Hugh McKiernan, O.C.S.O., was elected the first abbot. To support themselves the monks began operating a farm and running a bakery. In the seventies the community expanded their work, establishing Monastery Breads and began marketing their popular and lucrative product throughout the Washington, D.C., area.

After the Second Vatican Council and the cultural turmoil brought on by the radicalism of the Sixties, like many other religious communities, the abbey went through a difficult period with several monks leaving and fewer novices entering or staying. With their declining numbers and aging members, in 1990 it was decided to discontinue Monastery Breads, though the abbey has continued to sell fruit cakes successfully with use of both the internet and direct mail. Adaptive to changing times, in the Nineties the monks again expanded their work, becoming involved with a for-profit company. The firm, Electronic Scriptorium, farmed out data entry work to the monks who began digitizing card catalogues for universities such as Yale and Johns Hopkins. Reminiscent of the Middle Ages when monks earned their keep by copying manuscripts by hand, these modern monks see themselves to be sharing in the noble tradition of handing down learning by preserving data, but now in a high-tech form.

Today twenty-five monks, who range in age from twenty-five to eighty, live and work at Holy Cross Abbey. Though these men observe a quite strict form of religious life, they see themselves to be very much a part of the diocese of Arlington. The monastery chapel is almost always open to visitors who wish to participate in Mass or observe of the hours of prayer which the monks pray publicly, and for Sunday Mass, the chapel is often packed with Catholics from the surrounding area. The abbey maintains a separate facility for both men and women seeking to make a retreat and can accommodate up to fifteen retreatants at a time.

Left: Founded in 1950, today twenty-five Cistercian monks live at Holy Cross Abbey. (Photo: Bonnie Jacobs)

Right: In addition to assembling for Mass, Cistercian monks gather in the chapel five more times daily to pray the Liturgy of the Hours. (Photo: Algerina Perna)

In 1906 Joseph and Annie Dieken deeded a lot on the corner of Boundary Street and Lossing Avenue in Colonial Beach for the construction of St. Elizabeth Church. Quickly parishioners constructed a frame church, which was used until 1963.

Bishop Peter Leo Ireton, ninth Bishop of Richmond (1945-1958).

The Pentagon was built during World War II for thousands of workers, both military and civilian, who were organizing and supporting the war effort. Though peace came in 1945, many of these men and women remained to manage America's armed forces during the long Cold War. This permanently expanded military bureaucracy brought thousands of jobs and families to Northern Virginia.

1945. With this, Ireton became the ninth Bishop of Richmond. *At the beginning of his administration in 1935, Bishop Ireton had charge of a diocese with fifty-eight parishes* and fifty-four missions served by 120 priests, 23 of whom belonged to religious orders. Over the next eighteen years the number of parishes would increase to eighty-nine and the clergy would more than double. Even more dramatically, the Catholic population would almost triple in size. *By 1953 it had grown from around 35,000 to over 103,000.*

The expansion of government under the New Deal, as well as the increase in the size of military administrative structures that came during the Second World War and the Cold War, were responsible for much of the growth that had come to Northern Virginia by the forties and fifties. In his history of the Diocese of Richmond, Father Fogarty reminds his readers that this expansion of government was so colossal that it prompted one senator to call for the District of Columbia's re-annexation of the part of Virginia it had given up in 1847.

Although nothing ever came of this proposal, some, including Bishop Ireton, were troubled by its very discussion. The bishop realized that if Arlington and Alexandria were separated from Virginia and incorporated into the District, they would become part of the Archdiocese of Washington. This relatively small area accounted for fully one-sixth of the entire Catholic population of his diocese. Although no change took place at the time, to either the District's or the diocese's boundaries, thirty years later there would be realignment of diocesan boundaries. The new Diocese of Arlington that would emerge from the change would actually have a larger Catholic population than the Diocese of Richmond from which it had been carved.

In the last decades of the twentieth century, many American bishops had the unfortunate task of closing churches because of declining congregations. *By contrast, after the Second World War, Bishop Ireton was faced with the happy responsibility of opening new parishes.* The Northern Virginia suburbs of Washington saw their churches more than double. By 1957 there were nineteen parishes with resident pastors in Alexandria, Fairfax and Arlington alone. This included the establishment in 1946 of Our Lady Queen of Peace in Arlington, a parish for African American Catholics who were unwelcome in other area churches.

So many parishes had been founded in the years after the war that the deanery (an administrative division of a diocese) of Northern Virginia was split into two jurisdictions with Route 50 as the dividing line. In addition, by the early 1960s, almost every parish in the area was operating its own parochial school to educate the huge number of school-age baby-boomers.

While diocesan priests served in a majority of the parishes in Northern Virginia, the diocese also had churches administered by several religious orders, including the Holy Ghost Fathers, the Stigmatine Fathers, the Oblates of St. Francis de Sales and Missionhurst priests. In addition to the religious-order priests who participated in active ministries, Northern Virginia acquired its first group of cloistered monks in 1950, the Order of the Cistercians of the Strict Observance, more commonly known as "Trappists." *Coming from Rhode Island, they obtained a large tract of land in Berryville* on which they opened a daughter foundation, naming it the "Monastery of the Holy Cross." One of twelve Trappist foundations in the United States, Holy Cross remains the only monastery for men in the Arlington diocese.

The 1950s also brought a new Catholic high school and the first Catholic college to Northern Virginia. In 1952 the Religious of the Sacred Heart of Mary started Marymount Junior College in Arlington as an extension of a small private academy, which they were already operating.

Above: On September 20, 1946, Mrs. Alice Moorman, turned the first spade of dirt marking the beginning of construction of Our Lady Queen of Peace, a parish for black Catholics in Northern Virginia. Bottom: St. Luke's School in McLean was constructed in 1962.

Catholic parents had few choices of Catholic secondary schools for their children. Until the late 1950s, parents who wanted their children to attend a Catholic high school were limited to either St. Mary's in Alexandria or Marymount in Arlington. However, both were small academies, charged a relatively high tuition and were open only to girls. Many families were sending both sons and daughters to one of the several Catholic high schools in Washington, but these students had to contend with a long commute each day. By the early 1950s, some Catholic parents believed that the time was ripe for Northern Virginia to have its own affordable Catholic high school.

Beginning in 1952 a group of priests and parents representing the Arlington parishes of St. Ann, St. Agnes, St. Charles, St. Thomas More, and St. James in Falls Church began laying the plans for a high school. They soon found wide support, and in one year alone, the planners raised over a million dollars toward construction. *In 1958 their goal was finally achieved with the opening of Bishop Denis J. O'Connell High School in Arlington. Its student body then numbered four hundred.*

Although Bishop O'Connell High School admitted both boys and girls, it was not co-educational in the contemporary sense of the term.

Dedicated in 1958, the original Our Lady of Angels Church had 230 parishioners. Today the parish, which in 1985 built a much larger church, has more than 8,000 registered members.

As with the growing number of co-educational Catholic high schools around the country in the fifties, the boys and girls at Bishop O'Connell were taught in separate classes. Over time, this division by sex was ended. In its early years, the school had been staffed by I.H.M. Sisters for the girls and by the Brothers of the Christian Schools for the boys. In the school's first year of operation, only two laymen served on the faculty. As the number of women and men religious declined in the late 1960s

Bishop John J. Russell, the tenth Bishop of Richmond, presided at the 1963 groundbreaking for Bishop Ireton High School in Alexandria.

Marymount University:

Built as a summer home for Admiral Presley Rixey, Main House has been used for various purposes after the RSHM sisters purchased the property in 1948. Today, it is used for receptions and large gatherings.

*B*y the middle of the twentieth century, 224 Catholic colleges and universities were in operation in the United States. However, only one was located in Virginia. Overwhelmingly Protestant, at that time the state's population was less than three percent Roman Catholic. Despite the relatively small community from which to draw potential students, in 1950 a group of six Religious (sisters) of the Sacred Heart of Mary (RSHM) began Marymount Junor College in Arlington. Founded as a two-year institution for women, the school had an opening student body of thirteen. Today more than three thousand men and women are enrolled in both undergraduate and graduate programs. Considering its humble beginnings, Marymount, which in 1986 became a university, has achieved great success.

The founding of Marymount was the brainchild of Bishop Peter L. Ireton, the ninth Bishop of Richmond. Prompted by the postwar Baby Boom, he wanted to establish a Catholic high school for girls to rival the several

elite academies operated by the Episcopal Church, a pillar of old Virginian society. With this goal in mind, Ireton needed to find a group of women religious willing to start and staff the school. Though religious vocations were quite bountiful at this time, it was still not easy for a bishop to convince a religious order to accept such a large commitment of funds and personnel in the operation of a school. That is where Father Justin D. McClunn came in. He had a cousin who was an RSHM sister, and with this connection, Mother Gerard Phelan, superior general of the community, agreed to send a few sisters to open a school for girls. With some help from the diocese, the congregation took out a mortgage to purchase several buildings on a seventeen-acre site in Arlington. The property had been the estate of Admiral Presley M. Rixey, surgeon general under President Theodore Roosevelt.

In September 1948 Marymount Academy opened as a four-year high school and the next year the sisters added an elementary department. It had never been the intention

Then and Now

of Mother Gerard to have her sisters running a college in Virginia, especially since she already had her hands full in trying to staff Marymount College in Tarrytown, New York. However, once again Bishop Ireton had an idea. After speaking with Marymount's graduating seniors who told him how much they loved their school and how sad they were to have to leave it, Ireton asked Mother Gerard to begin a junior college. And once again demonstrating her congregation's generosity, Mother Gerard agreed to the bishop's request. The sisters' new endeavor quickly proved itself a success, and in 1952 the college graduated its first class.

Almost immediately, plans were made to expand the course of studies and to enlarge the physical plant to accommodate the needs of a college. During the presidency of Sister Berchmans Walsh, RSHM (1955-1960), the college took a made a step forward by gaining academic accreditation from the Southern Association of Colleges and Schools, an important accomplishment if an institution desires credibility from the wider academic community. This commitment to growth and the raising of intellectual standards continued and was strengthened during the tenure of the college's third president, Sister M. Majella Berg, RSHM (1960-1993).

Under Sister Majella's direction, in 1966 the college added both a nursing major and a foreign study program. In an effort to attract students from a population whose numbers had begun to decline dramatically by the early seventies, in 1973 Marymount became a four-year institution offering bachelor's degrees in twenty fields of study. This expansion to a four-year institution was a success, and by 1980 the school's enrollment had reached one thousand. In 1987 Marymount reinvented itself once

Mother M. Gerard Phelan was the superior general of the RSHM congregation who agreed to Bishop Ireton's request to open a school in Northern Virginia.

Sister M. Majella Berg, RSHM, served as president of Marymount from 1960 to 1993. Today she is chancellor of the university.

again and opened all its undergraduate programs to men. (Previously men were admitted only to the nursing program.) Though some regretted the loss of the school's original identity as a women's college, the development into a fully co-educational institution has been an overwhelming success. In an effort to reach Northern Virginia's expanding population which was moving farther west, in 1990 satellite campuses were opened in Sterling and Ballston.

After thirty-three years of leadership, Sister Majella stepped down from the office of president. However, she did not go into retirement. Today Sister Majella serves as the university's chancellor and continues to remain in daily contact with students by living in one of the undergraduate dormitories. In 1993 Marymount's board of trustees appointed Sister Eymard Gallagher, RSHM, as the school's fourth president. Over the past eight years, Sister Eymard has overseen the establishment of the Center for Ethical Concerns and the foundation of the university's first endowed Chair. In 1999 a new addition came to the campus with the opening of the Rose Benté Lee Center, which houses a 1,000-seat sports arena, a café, the university bookstore and several large meeting spaces.

In June 2001 Sister Eymard left to work for her congregation in New York. Due to the few sisters still engaged in higher education, the board of trustees sought an individual committed to running the university in the spirit of the motto of the RSHM sisters: _Ut Vitam Habeant_ ("That they may have life"). The first layman to lead the university, James E. Bundschuh, was appointed in July 2001 to serve as the fifth president. Dr. Bundschuh is dedicated to preserving Marymount's Catholic traditions and values as well as its academic excellence.

A young Oblate priest-teacher and some students at Bishop Ireton High School in the late 1960s.

and 1970s, Catholic lay men and women began to take their place. By the end of the 1990s, lay teachers at Bishop O'Connell had increased to almost one hundred. The size of the student body had also expanded dramatically. In 1999, Bishop O'Connell enrolled 1,400 students.

In addition to the joy and promise that marked the 1958 opening of the first diocesan high school in Northern Virginia, the year is remembered for the sadness it brought to the people of the Richmond diocese at the death of their beloved Bishop Ireton in April. Unlike the long interregnum that ensued after the passing of Richmond's first bishop, Rome now took quick action. On September 30, 1958, Bishop John J. Russell, formerly the Bishop of Charleston, South Carolina, was installed as the tenth Bishop of Richmond. Ordained a priest of the Archdiocese of Baltimore, he became a priest in Washington after the nation's capital was separated from Baltimore and made its own diocese in 1939. However, this was not to be Father Russell's last experience in the division of a diocese.

From the start of his administration, Bishop Russell continued the institutional expansion of the Richmond diocese that had begun after the Second World War. In 1959 the new bishop announced plans to open a high school seminary for boys. Until then, young men from the Richmond diocese who wanted to begin studies for the priesthood in high school had had to enroll in schools in other states. However, that changed in September 1960 with the opening of St. John Vianney Seminary. Unfortunately, financial problems closed St. John's in 1978.

In addition to his concern for the education of future priests, in 1960 Bishop Russell announced plans to build three new high schools in the diocese, two of which were to be in Northern Virginia. Because of the decline in religious vocations and the concomitant higher costs of hiring lay faculty, only one of the proposed schools ever actually opened. In 1968 Bishop Ireton High School began operation in Alexandria. Staffed by Oblates of St. Francis de Sales, the school was originally for boys, but with the closing of St. Mary's High School in Alexandria, Bishop Ireton was made co-ed in 1990. By 2000 it had an enrollment of about 900 students.

With his coming to Richmond, Bishop Russell was quickly faced with the pastoral challenges of dealing with the rapidly growing Catholic population of Northern Virginia. As the advance of the railroad had settled a small number of Catholics in Northern Virginia in the nineteenth century, the spread of the interstate highway system in the 1950s brought growth

Bishop John Russell of Richmond dedicated St. Thomas à Becket Church, Reston, in 1973.

of unimagined proportions. Once-sleepy villages like McLean, Reston and Vienna became bustling suburbs with their residents using the newly constructed Interstates 66, 95 and 495 to travel to their jobs in Washington, Maryland or other parts of the state. *Between 1958 and 1974, Bishop Russell presided over the opening of more than a dozen new parishes in Northern Virginia.* It was in recognition of this unprecedented growth, which was expected only to continue indefinitely, that serious discussion arose about the creation of a separate diocese for the region.

By the end of the 1960s, the growth of the Catholic population in Virginia had reached such proportions that for the first and only time Rome appointed a second auxiliary bishop to Richmond, and on December 1, 1970, Father Walter F. Sullivan was consecrated a bishop. Ordained a priest for the Richmond diocese in 1953, the new bishop had most recently served as chancellor as well as rector of the cathedral.

In December 1972, Bishop Russell turned seventy-five and submitted his resignation to Pope Paul VI. Before the Second Vatican Council (1962-65), ordinaries usually remained in office until their death. This changed in the late 1960s when Pope Paul VI instituted a retirement age for diocesan bishops. Russell stayed on as bishop of Richmond for two more years before his resignation was formally accepted. *On June 6, 1974, Bishop Sullivan replaced him, becoming the eleventh Bishop of Richmond and the last one whose jurisdiction included the entire state.*

The Garwood Whaley Auditorium at Bishop Ireton High School.

St. Francis of Assisi, Triangle

The Creation of the Diocese of Arlington

Bishop Thomas J. Welsh (1974-83)

Only days before Sullivan became the Bishop of Richmond, Rome promulgated *Supernae Christifidelium*, the papal bull that established the Diocese of Arlington. At the same time, the Vatican also announced the nomination of Bishop Thomas J. Welsh to be the first Bishop of Arlington. Ordained in 1946 for the Archdiocese of Philadelphia, Welsh worked in a variety of ministries including pastoral work and secondary school education. At the time of his episcopal ordination in 1970, Welsh was rector of St. Charles Borromeo Seminary in Overbrook, a suburb of Philadelphia. He remained in this position while also serving as an auxiliary bishop under John Cardinal Krol, the Archbishop of Philadelphia.

In late May 1974, shortly before the official announcement of the new diocese, Cardinal Krol privately informed Bishop Welsh of his new assignment. After breaking the news, Krol asked the new ordinary how he felt. Still a bit shocked by the unexpected announcement, Welsh replied that he would have to think about it. The Cardinal teasingly reminded Welsh that he, like the future-priests he was in charge of training, was ordained for service to the Church. Welsh smiled in agreement and the two began discussing Welsh's replacement at the seminary. After finishing the academic term in early July, Bishop Welsh came down to Northern Virginia to begin preparations for the new diocese.

On August 13, 1974, nearly forty bishops, dozens of priests and several hundred lay people gathered in the Cathedral of St. Thomas More in Arlington to attend the Mass of Installation of Bishop Welsh. In addition to the many bishops and priests who had come to show support to the new ordinary, two members of the hierarchy were there in an official capacity. Archbishop Jean Jadot, the apostolic delegate, came as the papal representative, and

Bishop Thomas J. Welsh, first Bishop of Arlington (1974-1983).

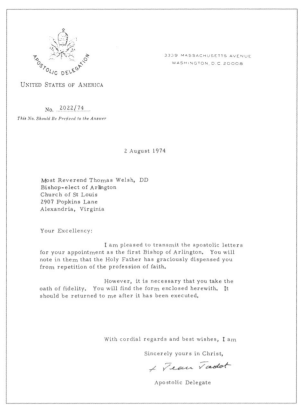

3339 MASSACHUSETTS AVENUE
WASHINGTON, D.C 20008

UNITED STATES OF AMERICA

No. _2022/74_
This No. Should Be Prefixed to the Answer

2 August 1974

Most Reverend Thomas Welsh, DD
Bishop-elect of Arlington
Church of St Louis
2907 Popkins Lane
Alexandria, Virginia

Your Excellency:

I am pleased to transmit the apostolic letters
for your appointment as the first Bishop of Arlington. You will
note in them that the Holy Father has graciously dispensed you
from repetition of the profession of faith.

However, it is necessary that you take the
oath of fidelity. You will find the form enclosed herewith. It
should be returned to me after it has been executed.

With cordial regards and best wishes, I am

Sincerely yours in Christ,

+ Jean Jadot

Apostolic Delegate

One of the official letters received by Bishop Welsh before he took canonical possession of the new diocese.

Archbishop William Borders of Baltimore was there since Arlington would be a suffragan (subordinate) diocese under the Archdiocese of Baltimore in some ecclesiastical matters. The presence of these two archbishops served as a visible reminder of the relationship between the Arlington diocese and the universal Church.

Monsignor Richard J. Burke, rector of the cathedral, read the papal decree that formally appointed Bishop Welsh to Arlington. In it Pope Paul VI described the bishop as diligent, prudent and pastoral. Later in the ceremony, Archbishops Jadot and Borders jointly presented Welsh with a crozier (staff) which symbolized his new role as shepherd of the Catholics of Northern Virginia. At the end of Mass, Bishop Welsh asked God to make the new diocese a place of prayer for all people, and he especially asked the Lord's blessing on President Gerald Ford who had just recently come into office.

At the time of its creation, the Diocese of Arlington contained fifty parishes which were served by sixty-six diocesan priests. In addition, there were ninety religious order priests in the diocese. However,

this second number included the monks at Berryville and other clergy who were not engaged in parochial ministry. Thus the new diocese was in real need of more priests. In comparison to other dioceses on the east coast, Arlington had a high priest-to-parishioner ratio, and, as with all Virginia's past bishops, Bishop Welsh would have to work hard to increase the number of priests. Toward this end, he soon appointed Father Richard Ley as the first promoter of vocations in the diocese.

Even before his installation, Bishop Welsh met with a group of knowledgeable clergy and laity who began laying plans for a diocesan curia (administration). Some of these early organizers were appointed to official positions, including Monsignor Paul V. Heller (vicar general),

It is traditional that the coat of arms of a diocese be composed of both the diocesan seal (left) as well as the personal seal of the bishop (right). With each new bishop, the diocesan coat of arms is changed.

Left side: The ten circular stars represent the Commonwealth of Virginia, the tenth state to ratify the Constitution. The larger star and the crescent symbolize the Blessed Virgin Mary, the patroness of both the United States as well as the Diocese of Arlington. The red chevron recalls St. Thomas More, the patron of the cathedral. The national colors red, white and blue, are used to recall the diocese's close proximity to Washington, D.C.

Right side: The Welsh (Walsh) family coat of arms was personalized by Bishop Welsh in his placement of a lance head on the red chevron between two black arrows. (St. Thomas the Apostle, Bishop Welsh's patron saint, is known by the spearhead upon which he was martyred.) The crowned "humilitas" recalls the coat of arms of St. Charles Borromeo, the patron of the seminary Welsh had previously headed.
Bishop Welsh's episcopal motto is translated: With Mary as model, make all things new.
The pontifical hat and the six green tassels symbolize the office of bishop.

Monsignor Richard J. Burke (chancellor) and Monsignor Justin D. McClunn (officialis).

In addition to these clerical appointments, in 1975 Bishop Welsh named Mr. Charles W. Carruth, as the founding editor of the *Arlington Catholic Herald*. For the first couple of years after the new diocese's creation, the *Catholic Virginian*, the newspaper of the Richmond diocese, had run a separate section devoted to the Arlington diocese. However, Bishop Welsh felt that Arlington should have its own newspaper to help forge a strong and separate identity for the Church in Northern Virginia. Carruth came to his new position after gaining extensive experience while working at the *Catholic News*, the newspaper of the Archdiocese of New York. The first issue of the *Herald* came out on January 8, 1976, and has been published on a weekly basis since. Carruth retired as editor in 1991 and was replaced by Mr. Michael F. Flach, the current editor and general manager. Mr. Flach had joined the paper in 1982 as a staff writer.

Mr. Carruth was not the only lay person to be a member of the first diocesan administration. On August 1 Mr. John (Jack) J. Connell was named the diocesan business manager, a position he held until his retirement in 1992. A long-time member of the cathedral parish, Mr. Connell died in 1999. In addition, a few women also held leadership positions during the early years of the new diocese. They include Mrs. Cathy Hlavin, president of the Council of Catholic Women and Mrs. Nancy Blanks, director of the Office of Social Development.

As far as the physical space in which to conduct the daily business of the chancery (administration), the diocese rented offices in a newly constructed building

4110 WARREN STREET, N.W.
WASHINGTON, D.C. 20016

June 13, 1974

His Excellency
The Most Reverend Thomas J. Welsh
Bishop-Elect of Arlington
St. Charles Borromeo Seminary
Philadelphia, Pennsylvania 19151

Your Excellency:

Please do accept my congratulations on your appointment as the first Bishop of Arlington in Virginia. The northern section of Virginia which becomes your new diocese has grown a great deal within the last fifteen years.

As you know it fell in my lap to set up the Archdiocese of Washington. It was indeed very interesting and I am sure you will find your experience in Arlington the same.

Please be assured of my prayers. May the good Lord bless you in your new assignment!

With cordial best wishes, I am

Faithfully yours in Christ,

+Patrick Cardinal O'Boyle

at 200 North Glebe Road. The property was adjacent to St. Thomas More Cathedral and had once been owned by the parish. In the beginning, most of the diocesan administration was located on the seventh floor of this office building. Over time, the chancery has spread out and now occupies three floors. Since it seemed more sensible to own rather than lease so much space, the diocese aquired the building in early 2001.

When Bishop Welsh first came to Arlington, he moved into the rectory at St. Thomas More. However, it is customary in many American dioceses for the bishop to live in a private residence unattached to the cathedral. So, in November 1974 the diocese purchased a two-story colonial house at 4600 North Carlyn Springs Road in Arlington to serve as the bishop's residence. Bishop Welsh and Father Ley, who in addition to his role as vocations director served as the bishop's secretary, moved into the house in December. The house has continued to be used as the residence of the ordinary of the diocese.

New Groups of Religious Sisters

*A*t the time of its establishment, Arlington had members of thirty-four religious congregations of *both men and women working in the diocese.* Almost all of these congregations were apostolic in that the members (priests, sisters, brothers) performed ministries to build up the Church while still living in accord with the rule of each respective community. The sole exception was Holy Cross Abbey in Berryville, which was the only truly monastic order in the diocese. At the time of the diocese's foundation, there was no cloistered monastic foundation for women. However, by 1977 Bishop Welsh and Msgr. McClunn were about to change that.

At the request of Bishop Welsh, in July 1977 Mother Mary Francis, the abbess of the Poor Clare Monastery of Our Lady of Guadalupe in Roswell, New Mexico, sent six nuns to start a cloister in Northern Virginia. The group first settled in St. Louis Church in Alexandria in the parish convent which had recently been vacated by the Franciscan Sisters of Allegany, N.Y. They remained here until February 1979 when they moved into a newly-constructed monastery on a six-acre parcel of land set back from the main highway. The property had been owned by the parish, and there had once been some thought to build a new church on it. However, it was eventually decided to build the church in another location and to construct the new monastery there instead. The sisters placed their new home under the protection of "Mary, Mother of the Church."

Since Poor Clare nuns are members of a mendicant (begging) order, the sisters have no way to support themselves. Like St. Francis and St. Clare of Assisi, founders of the order, these sisters depend on the kindness of others for their sustenance. Since first coming to the diocese, they have received generous support from the people of the Arlington diocese.

The monastery chapel is open for much of the day, and visitors are welcome to attend daily Mass or parts of the Liturgy of the Hours (the public prayer of the Church which all priests and some religious pray in common). People often stop by for a few minutes of prayer and the sisters welcome requests for prayer. The monastery has grown considerably since its foundation twenty-four years ago. Today the convent is home to seventeen nuns several of whom are native to Northern Virginia.

The Poor Clares were not the only new group of sisters to enter the diocese in the late seventies. In response to an invitation by Bishop Welsh, in 1978 two members of the Religious of the Cenacle came to open a house of prayer. This historically small congregation was founded in France in 1826 with the special purpose of conducting retreats and offering spiritual direction. In 1892 the first group of sisters emigrated to the U.S. The sisters who settled in Northern Virginia opened the first "Cenacle" in McLean before soon moving it to Vienna. At present the Cenacle house of prayer is located in Great Falls. A sole sister continues the community's ministry by leading individuals in various forms of the *Spiritual Exercises* of St. Ignatius Loyola as well as visiting local parishes to conduct group retreats.

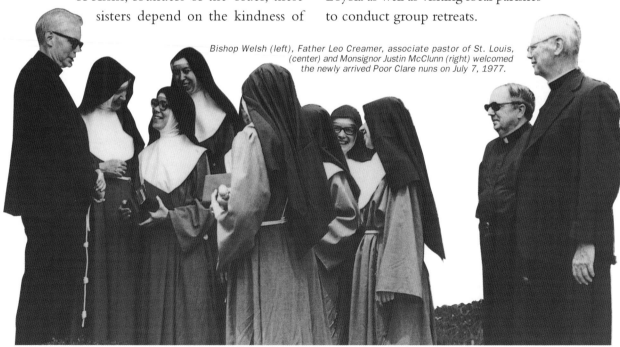

Bishop Welsh (left), Father Leo Creamer, associate pastor of St. Louis, (center) and Monsignor Justin McClunn (right) welcomed the newly arrived Poor Clare nuns on July 7, 1977.

In addition to the communities mentioned above, Bishop Welsh welcomed several other groups of women religious to the diocese. These include the Daughters of St. Paul who operate a Catholic bookstore and media center in Alexandria; the Dominican Sisters from Nashville who teach in the Aquinas School in Woodbridge; and the Vocation Sisters from England who are no longer present in the diocese. The bishop also supported an attempt to found a new community. Under the inspiration and leadership of Sister Joan Noreen Testa, a former member of the Sisters of St. Joseph of Chestnut Hill, Pennsylvania, the diocese sponsored "Our Lady's Missionaries of the Eucharist" as a "pious union" (the first stage in the canonical process to become a full-fledged religious community). Although the group did not become an independent religious community for women, it has grown to become a Church-approved lay association. Its members, single or married, dedicated themselves to a life of regular prayer and attendance at daily Mass as well as involvement in efforts at evangelization. Today Our Lady's Missionaries have members in Virginia, Pennsylvania and New Jersey.

Other New Beginnings

In an effort to support lay spirituality, in 1980 the Brent Society was formed and named in memory of Virginia's first Catholic family. The Society is dedicated to forging fellowship among Catholic leaders in business and the professions as they reflect on their vocation of living the Gospel in the midst of the world. Bishop Welsh was responsible for encouraging the society's foundation, and the organization remains under the spiritual direction of the Bishop of Arlington.

Besides sponsoring seminars and discussion groups for its membership, the group hosts the annual dinner during which the Bishop of Arlington awards the "Brent Distinguished Service Award" to honor a Catholic outstanding in service to the community. Originally called the "Brent Award for Distinguished Service to Fellowman" at the time of its establishment in 1976, Mildred F. Jefferson, M.D., founder of National Right to Life, was the award's first recipient. Recent honorees have included Senator Rick Santorum of Pennsylvania, Father Joseph Fessio, S.J., director of Ignatius Press, and the Honorable Antonin Scalia, associate justice of the Supreme Court.

While other American bishops were being forced to close churches in urban areas because of dwindling congregations, *Bishop Welsh had the happy duty of establishing a total of six new parishes during his nine years in Arlington.* New parishes came to Middleburg, Lake Ridge, Madison, Great Falls, Reston, and Arlington. These new starts included Holy Martyrs of Vietnam Parish, which was established in 1976 to serve the several thousand Vietnamese who had come to the diocese after the end of the Vietnam War. Earlier in 1975, Bishop Welsh had opened the Office of Migration and Refugee Services to care for the growing number of Hispanic and Asian immigrants who were moving to Northern Virginia. This office continues to aid immigrants by offering emergency housing and clothing, English as a Second Language (ESL) classes and employment services.

After more than eight years of service to the Catholics of Northern Virginia, on February 8, 1983, Bishop Welsh was appointed the second Bishop of Allentown, Pennsylvania. Although he was not returning to his native Philadelphia archdiocese, in many ways Bishop Welsh was returning home. He was born and raised in the area that was to become the Diocese of Allentown after its separation from the Philadelphia archdiocese in 1961. Bishop Welsh spent fourteen years as Bishop of Allentown before his retirement in 1997.

Diocesan Development

Bishop John R. Keating (1983-98)

After the announcement of Bishop Welsh's transfer, the College of Consultors of the diocese met and according to canonical procedure, selected Monsignor John P. Hannan to be diocesan administrator until the installation of a new bishop. Msgr. Hannan's term as administrator would be brief, for on June 7, 1983, it was officially announced that Pope John Paul II had named Father John R. Keating, chancellor and vicar general of the Archdiocese of Chicago, to be the second Bishop of Arlington. Bishop-elect Keating soon contacted Msgr. Hannan to lay plans for his arrival in Arlington. *On August 4, 1983, he was both ordained to the episcopacy and officially installed as Bishop of Arlington.*

Born in Chicago in 1934, John Richard Keating attended Quigley Preparatory Seminary and St. Mary of the Lake Seminary (Mundelein) before going to Rome to complete his studies for the priesthood at the Jesuit-run Gregorian University. Ordained in 1958, he worked briefly as a parish priest in Chicago before returning to Rome in 1963 to earn a doctorate in canon law, again studying at the Gregorian. Keating held chancery positions under both Albert Cardinal Meyer and John Cardinal Cody while also serving as an associate pastor in several Chicago-area parishes. After Cody's death in 1982, he was elected administrator of the archdiocese until the installation of then-Archbishop Joseph Bernadin. Father Keating served briefly under Bernadin as vicar general and chancellor before his transfer to Arlington.

These two new ordinaries, Bishop Keating and Archbishop Bernadin, took the helm of two local churches (Northern Virginia and Chicago), which were facing very different challenges. During his fourteen years as archbishop, Cardinal Bernadin was forced to close and consolidate several dozen urban and ethnic parishes and deal with the grief and anger associated with this reorganization. In contrast, during his fifteen years in Arlington, Bishop Keating had the happy task of presiding over the continuing growth of the Catholic population in his diocese and planning the expansion in the number of parishes, schools and other ministries. This atmosphere of hope and growth greeted the new bishop from the moment of his arrival.

In a series of articles in the *Arlington Catholic Herald* chronicling the development of the Arlington diocese during its first twenty-five years, Father Thomas P. Ferguson noted that less than twenty-four hours after his installation, Bishop Keating was busy presiding over the dedication of a new parish church. And this practice of blessing

The Chancery staff gathered outside St. Thomas More Cathedral to wish Bishop Welsh well as he departed to become the Bishop of Allentown, Pennsylvania.

new buildings was just beginning. *During his tenure, Keating would dedicate twenty churches and open seven new schools.* In addition, he established six new parishes: Sacred Heart, Manassas (1984); St. Andrew the Apostle, Clifton (1989); St. Theresa, Ashburn (1991); St. Paul Chung, Fairfax (1996); St. Clare of Assisi, Clifton (1996); and St. Raymond of Penafort, Fairfax Station (1997).

Expansion in Catholic Secondary Education

*O*n September 27, 1985, Bishop Keating presided over the formal dedication of Paul VI High School in Fairfax. However, this ceremony did not mark the beginning of the school, which actually had begun operation two years earlier. In 1980 Bishop Welsh gave approval for plans to establish a new diocesan high school because of long waiting lists at both Bishop O'Connell High School and Bishop Ireton High School. In addition, both these older schools were located inside the Beltway, and since much of the

new growth in the region was coming to the western part of Fairfax County, it was decided that if a new school were established, it should be located farther west. In 1982 the Oblates of St. Francis de Sales agreed to staff the new school, and four Oblates were part of the first faculty that included more than two dozen lay teachers.

In December 1982 the diocese purchased the former Fairfax High School on Lee Highway for $2.2 million and began laying plans for its

The diocesan coat of arms under Bishop Keating.
Like Bishop Welsh's coat of arms, the left side of the insignia was taken from the diocesan seal. The right is reserved to the individual bishop's heraldry. Bishop Keating used a variation on his family's coat of arms in the creation of his own. The red saltair ("X") has two green nettles like his family's but above Keating placed an eagle's head, the traditional symbol of St. John the Evangelist, his baptismal patron. The anchor was taken from the coat of arms of St. Pius X, a hero of Bishop Keating.
Bishop Keating's episcopal motto was taken from St. Paul's Letter to the Colossians (2:7).

BE ROOTED IN HIM

transformation into the new Paul VI High School. At the time of the sale, the facility was being used as an annex for George Mason University, and the former occupant vacated the building in June 1983. Father Donald J. Heet, O.S.F.S., the school's founding principal and his staff performed a minor miracle in readying the facilities for the opening of school in less than two months. On August 30, 1983, their hard work paid off, and classes began for more than 350 boys and girls. By 1985 the enrollment had topped 950, and the next year the school graduated its first class of 120 students.

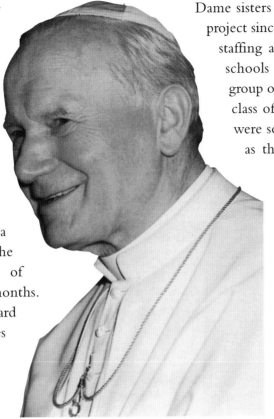

Pope John Paul II appointed Bishop Keating to the Diocese of Arlington in 1983.

Dame sisters to consider taking on this project since they were so successful in staffing and running several parish schools in Northern Virginia. A group of seven girls formed the first class of the new school, and they were soon joined by many others as the school began admitting both boarding and day students.

Sensitive to the changing needs of the local community, in September 1990 the school became co-educational and dis-continued its boarding program. In 2000 Notre Dame had an enrollment of over 230 girls and boys in grades nine through twelve with some students commu-

After much consideration and a good bit of regret, in 1999, the Oblate superiors announced that because of the declining vocations, the community would withdraw from the school. The last Oblates left at the end of the 1999-2000 academic year. On July 1, 2000, Mr. Philip V. Robey became the first lay principal and the school currently enrolls more than 1,200 students. The withdrawal of the Oblates from Paul VI did not represent a complete departure of the Oblates from the Arlington diocese. The community still has members working at Bishop Ireton High School and continues to staff Our Lady of Good Counsel Parish in Vienna and St. John Neumann Parish in Reston.

In April 1990, Bishop Keating traveled to the western part of the diocese to help celebrate the twenty-fifth anniversary of Notre Dame Academy in Middleburg. The high school was founded in 1965 by the Sisters of Notre Dame of Chardon, Ohio, in response to an invitation by Bishop Russell. The bishop wanted a girls' boarding school in this part of the diocese and asked the Notre

ting up to thirty-five miles each way. Although the school is no longer owned by the Sisters of Notre Dame but by a lay Board of Trustees with a formal relationship to the Arlington diocese, three sisters remain active at the school. Notre Dame remains the only Catholic high school in the western part of diocese and anticipates continued growth as the suburbs of Washington push farther in its direction. With the projection of these demographics, the school is in process of upgrading its athletic fields and making plans to convert some auxiliary buildings for faculty housing and administration.

Besides supporting Catholic schools sponsored by the diocese or religious orders, Bishop Keating also encouraged the start or expansion of several private, lay-owned Catholic schools. In 1991 he dedicated a new wing at Seton School in Manassas. Founded in 1975 by lay persons, the school currently enrolls 350 boys and girls in grades seven through twelve. Although it is not sponsored by the diocese, the school maintains an official affiliation with the Church. Its religion teachers hold diocesan certification.

Christendom College

*D*isappointed with the changes that came to American Catholic higher education in the late sixties, in 1977 a group led by Warren H. Carroll, Ph.D., launched Christendom College to offer a "truly liberal arts education...to maintain the idea of Christendom." Since its beginning with twenty-six undergraduates in rented space in the former St. Francis of Assisi School in Triangle, the institution has grown to enroll over three hundred students in its undergraduate and graduate departments. In 1979 the college moved to its present seventy-two-acre campus in Front Royal, which was formerly owned by the AFL-CIO.

In 1997 Christendom merged with the Notre Dame Institute of Alexandria to become the Notre Dame Graduate School of Christendom College. Originally founded in 1969 by the Sisters of Notre Dame of Chardon, Ohio, who also founded Notre Dame Academy in Middleburg, the newly formed institution grants masters' degrees in theological studies with courses offered at both campuses. Since 2000 the college has raised over $8.5 million in gifts and bequests and hopes to find more suitable space for its Alexandria campus which continues to expand.

With the help of Bishop Welsh, Christendom was able to obtain a campus in Front Royal in 1979.

Death of Bishop Keating

*D*uring his tenure as leader of the Church in Northern Virginia, Bishop Keating ordained eighty-four men to the priesthood. In the last decades of the twentieth century, few other American bishops have seen so great a number of priestly vocations. This increase in the presbyterate was critically needed since the Catholic population grew from 188,000 at the time of Keating's installation in 1983 to more than 336,000 at the time of his death in 1998.

Given that he was in good health and just 63 years old, *Bishop Keating's death on March 22, 1998, came as a shock to the people of the Arlington diocese.* The bishop died after suffering a massive heart attack while on an *ad limina* visit in Rome with other bishops from the Mid-Atlantic. (Canon law requires that all bishops visit with the pope every five years.) His body was flown back to Arlington and a public wake was held in the cathedral on March 27.

During a prayer service that evening, James Cardinal Hickey, the Archbishop of Washington, praised Bishop Keating for his "fidelity to the teaching of the apostles" and devotion to the Mass.

The Cardinal also offered some personal memories of the late bishop, including his graciousness, sense of humor and love of golf. In a special issue of the *Arlington Catholic Herald* dedicated to the memory of the late bishop, others spoke of their remembrances of Bishop Keating. Sister Patrick Marie Doherty, I.H.M., who worked at the diocesan chancery, praised Keating's commitment to Catholic education and concern for Arlington's growing Hispanic community. The offering of kind words about the deceased leader was not limited to priests and religious. Jon Yauger, a student at Marymount University, commented on the impact Keating's "sound advice and opinions" had made on his personal and moral development.

On March 28 at St. Thomas More Cathedral in Arlington, more than two thousand mourners participated in the Mass of Christian Burial for Bishop Keating celebrated by William Cardinal Keeler, Archbishop of Baltimore, and scores of bishops and priests. In the homily delivered by long-time friend and fellow Chicago priest, Bishop

Parishes with large congregations are common in the diocese, especially in Fairfax and Loudoun Counties. At Our Lady of Good Counsel Parish, Vienna, Father John M. O'Neill, O.S.F.S. blesses palms outside on Palm Sunday before the congregation moves into the church for the rest of the liturgy.

Edward M. Egan, then the head of the Diocese of Bridgeport, Connecticut, Egan stressed how much his late friend loved life in Rome where he had spent nine years in study. It was here that he honed his skills in canon law, becoming, according to Egan, a "world-class canonist." His skill in interpreting the finer points of church law won Keating a papal appointment to the Pontifical Commission of Legislative Texts in 1986. A first-rate administrator, Egan called Keating, who was most proud of the record number of ordinations the diocese had received during his tenure.

At the conclusion of the liturgy, Bishop Keating's body was given a temporary interment at Columbia Gardens Cemetery in Arlington. *On December 20, 1998 his remains were re-interred in a newly-constructed burial crypt in the cathedral.* The vault was built as a final resting-place for the bishops of Arlington and contains space for fifteen bodies.

A Young Diocese Enters a New Millenium

*A*s after the transfer of Bishop Welsh in 1983, the diocesan College of Consultors met after the death of Bishop Keating to select a diocesan administrator. On March 26, 1998, the eleven-member group of priests chose Monsignor James W. McMurtrie to lead the diocese. Ordained in 1962 as a priest of the Richmond diocese, Msgr. McMurtrie was then serving as pastor of St. Theresa Parish in Ashburn.

During the interregnum, McMurtrie oversaw the daily operations of the diocese and lent his support to projects already in process (including the construction of the crypt in the cathedral). In the spring he handled the changes in priest personnel and appointed several priests to the position of parish administrator. (According to canon law, only the diocesan bishop can name a new pastor.) One thing McMurtrie could not do was confer holy orders on seminarians who had completed their course of studies. However, the Arlington diocese had an old friend who was more than willing to lend a hand. In June 1998, Bishop Welsh returned

On December 20, 1998, Bishop Keating's remains were re-interred in the newly constructed burial crypt in St. Thomas More Cathedral.

and ordained three men to the priesthood at St. Thomas More Cathedral in Arlington.

After more than ten months of waiting, *on January 25, 1999, Pope John Paul II appointed Bishop Paul Stephen Loverde,* ordinary of the Diocese of Ogdensburg, New York, *as the third Bishop of Arlington.* Although Msgr. McMurtrie performed a fine job in holding things together in the absence of a regular bishop, there was a general sense of relief when word of the appointment arrived. It is never good for a local church to be without a regular bishop.

Born in 1940 in Framingham, Massachusetts, Bishop Loverde grew up and received his early education in Connecticut and Rhode Island. In 1958 he graduated from LaSalle Academy in Providence. He began studies for the priesthood for the Diocese of Norwich, Connecticut, at the former St. Thomas Seminary in Bloomfield. In 1962 Loverde completed an undergraduate degree at the former St. Bernard's Seminary College in Rochester, New York, before moving on to the Gregorian University in Rome to complete his studies for the priesthood.

In 1965 Loverde was ordained a priest and sent to St. Sebatian's Parish in Middletown as curate where he also did part-time campus ministry in a local college. In 1969 he was transferred to work in a Catholic high school while continuing with his ministry to college students. In 1974 Father Loverde became involved with work in the diocesan tribunal and the office of clergy personnel. From 1979 to 1981 he studied for a licentiate in canon law at the Catholic University of America and then was assigned as vice-officialis of the diocesan tribunal and in 1985 as the bishop's delegate for clergy.

In 1988, Father Loverde was ordained to the episcopacy and named an auxiliary bishop for the Archdiocese of Hartford. After little more than five years in Hartford, Pope John Paul II transferred Bishop Loverde to upstate New York where he became the eleventh Bishop of Ogdensburg, a largely rural diocese which borders Canada. Bishop Loverde was soon well loved by both the clergy and laity of this relatively small local church. (The Diocese of Ogdensburg covers almost twice the area as the Diocese of Arlington, but its Catholic population is less than half as large.) At news of his transfer, Bishop Loverde said that he was sad to be leaving the north country of New York State and its people who had impressed him by their "deep faith." However, he went on to acknowledge that he was excited by the new challenges that lay ahead in Northern Virginia.

Bishop Paul S. Loverde, third Bishop of Arlington.

The Challenge of Continued Growth

A story recounted in a recent article in the "Metro" section of the *Washington Post* exemplifies well the challenges that rapid growth has brought to the Church in Northern Virginia. Entitled, "Too Many Pupils, Too Few Desks," the *Post* writer described the problem faced by the Diocese of Arlington in trying to meet the need for more spaces in Catholic schools, which has arisen from an increase in the number of school-age children. *While the Catholic population has more than doubled since the founding of the diocese in 1974, the number of Catholic elementary schools has grown by less than 50 percent, expanding only from 25 to 35 percent.*

The strain at the secondary school level has been equally difficult. Here the number of high school slots has increased by only twenty-six percent. This lack of space has caused long waiting lists. For the freshman class to enter in the fall of 2001, Bishop O'Connell High School had 375 slots but 850 applicants. With the opening of Paul VI High

The diocesan coat of arms under Bishop Loverde.
With the installation of Bishop Loverde in 1999, the right side of the diocesan coat of arms again changed. Bishop Loverde chose a green field recalling that his Italian surname means "the green one." A white anchor, the symbol of hope, is laced with an "M," standing for Mary, the Mother of God. Bishop Loverde was named a bishop during the last Marian year, 1987-88. The silver star, recalling Polaris, the North Star, was chosen in recognition of the bishop's home diocese of Norwich, ("North Town") Connecticut.
The lower portion of the arms include blue and white wavy bars, a symbol taken from the arms of the Archdiocese of Hartford, where Loverde worked as an auxiliary bishop. These bars are also used to represent the Pawcatuck River and Loverde's hometown of the same name. Coming forth from the water are three gold hills to honor his Italian heritage. Bishop Loverde's father came from village of Pollina and his maternal grandparents came from the villages of Tusa and San Mauro-Castleverde, all close to each other in the hills of Sicily.
Bishop Loverde's episcopal motto is taken from St. Paul's Second Letter to Timothy (4:2).

Using an ancient rite of the Church, Bishop Loverde consecrated the new altar with holy oil at the newly constructed Christ the Redeemer, Sterling. In rear: Father C. Donald Howard, S.A., pastor.

School in 1983 the diocese had hoped to address the increased demand for Catholic education, but even the addition of 1,200 slots has not proved sufficient. This predicament has forced many parents to send their sons and daughters to Catholic schools outside the immediate area, mainly in the neighboring Archdiocese of Washington, and many have not been deterred by lengthy commutes. Almost one-third of the young men at Gonzaga College High School in Washington, D.C. live in the Arlington diocese, some students traveling from as far as Fredericksburg, forty miles to the south.

The dearth of places in Catholic schools has not been the only shortage faced by the diocese. Despite the fact that in recent years Arlington has been blessed with a good number of priestly vocations, especially in comparison to many other dioceses, there is still a need for more priests to meet the new demands of the larger Catholic population. Some of the parishes in Northern Virginia have grown incredibly large, a few with more than 10,000 registered parishioners. However, without an even larger number of new priests, it would not be feasible to open new parishes since there are just not enough priests to administer them.

In 1991, the Diocese of Arlington assumed responsibility for San Francisco de Asís in Bánica, the Dominican Republic. Bishop Keating appointed Father Gerard Creedon, formerly pastor of Good Shepherd Parish in Alexandria, as the first pastor. The diocese has also taken charge of San José Parish in Pedro Santana. Over the past ten years a strong relationship has been built between the Dominicans of these parishes and Catholics of the Arlington diocese with several men and women from Northern Virginia serving as volunteers in this very poor part of the world. In 1996 Tony Imhof, a parishioner of St. Ann Church in Arlington, spent several months teaching English to young people in the parish in Bánica. He also organized the area's only library.

Over the years, the diocese has often had the help of other bishops with confirmations since it is not easy for Arlington's sole bishop to celebrate this last sacrament of initiation himself in all sixty-six parishes. In the fall of 2000, Bishop John J. Kaising of the Archdiocese for Military Services visited St. Luke Parish in McLean to perform confirmations. After the liturgy Matthew Bresnahan (left), an eighth grader in St. Luke School, and Matthew Fizgerald, his uncle and sponsor, posed for a photo with the bishop.

Parish Section

CATHEDRAL OF ST. THOMAS MORE

When St. Thomas More Parish was started in 1938, it is doubtful that any of its founders knew that it would become the cathedral church of a new diocese in Northern Virginia. Although this change did come in 1974, it has continued to serve as a parish church for the people in its Arlington neighborhood, remaining true to the reason for its foundation. Unlike many dioceses whose cathedrals are in the downtown district, a business neighborhood often with few regular parishioners, Arlington's St. Thomas More Cathedral remains an active parish with a mix of people. The parish composition runs from young to old. There are aged, retired, an abundance of middle aged, as well as young professionals, with and without families. Not unlike most other parishes in Northern Virginia, it is a good example of a typical parish in the Diocese of Arlington.

Bells have long been used to mark time and call worshippers to prayer. They have also taken on a symbolic role in reminding all hearers of the continuous presence of God.

For more than twenty years before the construction of the present church in 1961, parishioners of St. Thomas More worshipped in a gymnasium and an auditorium in the school, which was built in 1944. Since it is quite close to Washington, D.C., Arlington was one of the first areas in Northern Virginia to experience rapid growth in the postwar era, and St. Thomas More shared in this expansion. The parish remains alive and sponsors more than thirty activities, including a group for stay-at-home mothers who meet to discuss how the teachings of the Church affect the lives of young families. Sensitive to the changing demographics of the area, the parish added a Spanish Mass in 1990 to accommodate Arlington's growing Hispanic population.

For the first fifty-two years of its existence, the St. Thomas More School was administered and partly staffed by the Immaculate Heart of Mary (I.H.M.) sisters. The school began with sixty kindergarteners with the first sisters traveling from the convent at St. James Parish in Falls Church and picking up several students along their commute. In 1997, the sisters regretfully announced the necessity of withdrawal from the school due to declining numbers and aging members. Although the sisters left with heavy hearts, they left behind a school that is now flourishing under lay leadership, with an excellent principal and staff. The school structure itself, in the last few years, has undergone many improvements, including air-conditioning and a new heating system to insure its future comfort well into the new millennium.

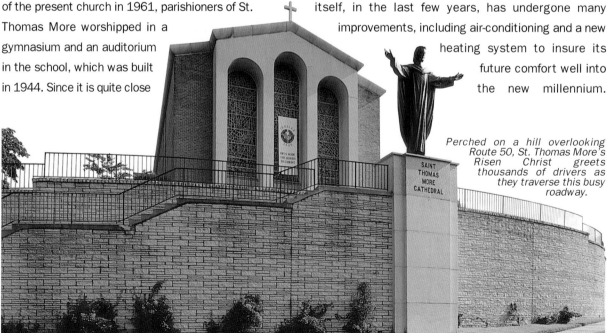

Perched on a hill overlooking Route 50, St. Thomas More's Risen Christ greets thousands of drivers as they traverse this busy roadway.

ARLINGTON

HOLY MARTYRS OF VIETNAM

Founded in 1979, Holy Martyrs of Vietnam was the first U.S. parish for Vietnamese Catholics. After the devastation that came as a result of so many years of war in their country, hundreds of thousands of Vietnamese left their homeland, especially those who fought for or supported the South Vietnamese government. With this exodus came several hundred Vietnamese to Northern Virginia. In July 1975, Father Tran Duy Nhat celebrated Mass at St. Thomas More Cathedral for the pilgrim Vietnamese immigrants. In many ways this liturgy marks the roots of Holy Martyrs of Vietnam Parish which was founded four years later. (Originally the parish was given the name, "Blessed Vietnamese Martyrs," but this was changed by Bishop Keating in 1989 after the canonization of 117 Vietnamese men and women who gave their lives for their faith more than three centuries ago.)

Since the Vietnamese population continued to grow in Northern Virginia during the last years of the 1970s, Bishop Welsh established a parish to serve the immigrants, many of whom were Catholic. (Before the Communist victory, Vietnam was about thirteen percent Roman Catholic.) At first, the new parish met in a former Protestant church in Annandale, but quickly its growing numbers required a larger space. In 1986 a loan from the diocese allowed Holy Martyrs to purchase the former Barcroft Bible Church in Arlington, which the parishioners helped to refurbish, incorporating an Asian theme in some of the furnishings and artwork. The larger space was sorely needed since today Holy Martyrs of Vietnam has grown to 4,400 parishioners.

In August 2000, Bishop Loverde turned the parish over to the pastoral care of the Order of Preachers (Dominicans) who have Vietnamese-speaking friars stationed in Arlington.

The choir at a celebration of the patronal feast of the parish.

Vietnamese Eucharistic Society of Holy Martyrs of Vietnam.

OUR LADY OF LOURDES

Founded in 1946, Our Lady of Lourdes Parish is in the densely populated Crystal City area of Arlington. Because the neighborhood is so close to Washington, D.C., and is served by the the Metro

system, the cost of buying or renting a home has risen greatly in recent years, and the high cost of living has kept away young families with small children. Thus in recent decades the parish has remained small (1,300 members) with a large population of senior citizens who have been in the neighborhood for many years as well as a good number of retired military personnel. Since Our Lady of Lourdes was never large enough to maintain its own parochial school, some of the children in the parish attend nearby Catholic schools in addition to Arlington County schools.

The main church, which is just off Route 1, was built in 1963. Before its completion, the lower part of Lourdes Center was used for Mass. Today the Center contains eight classrooms, which are used for religious education classes, an auditorium and a kitchen. Although many parishioners are in retirement, they have not ceased being active, and for several years now the parish has supported a

Left: Sanctuary of Our Lady of Lourdes.
Bottom: A modern brick structure, Our Lady of Lourdes Church is located near busy Route 1.

senior citizens group, which sponsors social, spiritual and community service activities for its members. The young people of Our Lady of Lourdes also maintain an active presence in the parish. They have formed a Young Adults Group and have helped to raise money for the parish Pro-Life Garden, which Bishop Loverde dedicated in September 1999. In addition, in recent years a Spanish Mass has been added to the Sunday schedule in response to the growing Hispanic community in Arlington.

In September 1999, Bishop Loverde celebrated a Sunday Mass at Our Lady of Lourdes and later dedicated the new Pro-Life Memorial Garden.

OUR LADY QUEEN OF PEACE

Unfortunately for many years black Catholics in America suffered injustices and discrimination, not only in society as a whole, but also within their very own Church. Until shortly before the Civil Rights era, blacks were unwelcome in many Catholic parishes, schools and hospitals. In the South they often had to sit in specially designated areas (usually in the rear of the church, or had to worship in separate all-black parishes. This ugly truth was also true for black Catholics in Arlington who had to take three buses to St. Joseph's, Alexandria, a parish founded for African Americans, or to a church in Washington, D.C., which had several black parishes. However, in 1945, 16 black Catholic families in Arlington decided to no longer tolerate being treated as second-class citizens. After receiving permission from Bishop Peter Ireton of Richmond, they laid plans to form Our Lady Queen of Peace (OLQP), a parish which would respect and affirm the dignity of African Americans.

At the founding of OLQP, Bishop Ireton invited the Holy Ghost Fathers to serve in the parish. At that time, this Order was one of the few American religious communities with experience in ministering to blacks. It was also one of the few to admit African-American candidates for the priesthood. For the first 18 years of its existence, the parish was without boundaries and any black Catholic in Northern Virginia could register as a parishioner.

As racial boundaries began to be broken down in the late 1950s and 1960s, OLQP was given formal boundaries like most other parishes. Today the parish has a mix of black, white and Hispanic members and numbers close to 1,900 parishioners. It regularly holds a Spanish Sunday liturgy.

From the beginning, the people of OLQP have had a strong commitment to advancing the cause of justice and serving those in need. Toward that end, the parish maintains a myriad of social service programs, including ministry to the poor, the homebound and people living with HIV and AIDS. Realizing that the Church has a special obligation to nurture children, OLQP operates an "Early Learning Center" program for children aged 2-6 with tuition based on family income. This concern and care for others has not been limited to people living in the Arlington area. In 1997 the parish also became twinned with a sister parish in Medor, Haiti, allowing OLQP's parishioners to learn more about the needs of the global community and the obligation to share the great wealth that many Americans enjoy.

Our Lady Queen of Peace Church was dedicated in 1947.

ST. AGNES

St. Agnes began as a mission of St. Charles Borromeo in 1914. For the first six years the parishioners worshipped in several different rented spaces, including a movie theater and grocery store. Six years later Bishop Peter Ireton dedicated the first permanent church, and in 1936 St. Agnes was eventually made an independent parish.

In 1946 a school was opened, and for many years was staffed by the Sisters of Notre Dame (Chardon, Ohio), the first of many parochial schools in Northern Virginia in which members of this congregation would come to serve. By the late 1950s, the enrollment hit an all-time high of 900. Today 394 students are in attendance.

To meet the needs of the parish and school as both continued to experience strong growth, in 1952 a new

Our Lady of Guadalupe is the patron saint of the Americas.

church and a new addition to the school were built. Again, not long afterwards, in 1966, another church was built and this building continues to serve the people of St. Agnes. Conscious of the need to share one's gifts, in 1965 a group of parishioners helped launch the "Brother Dennis" tithing program. After more than 35 years, it remains popular. Innovative in design and operation, the program donates a certain percentage of the donations made to the fund to a series of different charities that are rotated on a regular basis. The parish's web site contains the links to the different groups that benefit from the parishioners' stewardship. In 1987 the site of the original church was sold, and with the funds the Parish Center was constructed. In addition, improvements were made to the church and school buildings.

Since Arlington is already highly developed, no large-scale growth is expected in the parish as it is in other parishes farther west. However, St. Agnes remains large and active with more than 6,000 registered parishioners.

St. Agnes Church in Arlington.

ST. ANN

The origins of St. Ann's Parish go back to the era when Northern Virginia was still a part of the Diocese of Richmond. In 1941 Bishop Peter Ireton purchased property at the corner of Tenth and Frederick Streets in north Arlington with the intention of establishing a new parish some time in the near future. These plans came to fruition six years later with the official establishment of St. Ann's. The church was completed two years later, and in 1960, it was enlarged into its present cruciform shape.

In 1951 the parish began operating a school that was originally staffed by the Sisters of Loretto until their departure in 1964. They were replaced by the Sisters of Notre Dame (Chardon, Ohio) who have remained a presence in the school and church, though not in the same numbers as in the mid-1960s when the membership of American religious congregations had reached a zenith. Today the school enrolls 259 children and offers extended care and learning-disabled programs.

Reaching out to the wider community, the parish provides pastoral care for patients at nearby Arlington Hospital and Hospice of Northern Virginia. In addition to employing the ministry of parish priests, in recent years this hospital ministry has grown to include the Sisters of Notre Dame of the parish as well as parishioners who give of their time and compassion in visiting the sick. The parish also sponsors a Bereavement Committee that offers support to ease the pain of those who have recently lost a loved one.

In 1948 Charles Larmer and the former Sarah Slieglitz could not wait for the new St. Ann's Church to be completed. They were married in the church three weeks before the cornerstone was laid.

St. Ann's School opened in 1951. Sister Mary Campion, a Sister of Loretto, leads her first-grade class in prayer before the start of the first lesson.

St. Ann's Church in Arlington.

ST. CHARLES BORROMEO

The first parish in Arlington County, St. Charles Borromeo Parish was founded in 1909 by Bishop Augustine van de Vyver of Richmond. Plans were quickly made for the building of a church, and on March 16, 1911, Archbishop Diomede Falconio, the apostolic delegate to the American Church, presided over the dedication of the new structure.

As with many other parishes founded in the U.S. during this era, St. Charles Borromeo soon opened a school. In 1922 a four-classroom school was staffed by a group of Benedictine Sisters from Bristow, Virginia. A house on Lawton (now, Hudson) Street was bought and given to the sisters for a convent. With the huge increase in the school-age population after the Second World War, a new ten-room school was built along with a convent. This building continues to be used by the school, which now enrolls 240 students. Since 1976 Sister Benedict Kesock, O.S.B., has served as the school principal and is the only Benedictine sister still involved with the school.

Beginning in the 1960s, Arlington has witnessed a growing presence of Hispanics in its neighborhoods, especially on the south side of Route 50. In response to these new residents who traditionally have been overwhelmingly Catholic, in the early 1970s St. Charles Borromeo inaugurated a Spanish liturgy, one of the first in Northern Virginia. A popular liturgy, the Sunday Spanish Mass attracts a standing-room-only crowd, though several other parishes in Arlington also have liturgies in Spanish.

Committed to the promotion of justice, in 1988 the parish established Borromeo Housing in response to the rising number of homeless populating the city streets. Today Borromeo Housing

St. Charles Borromeo School.

Fr. Francisco Mendez de Dios, parochial vicar at St. Charles Borromeo, greets parishioners after a Sunday Mass during Advent in 1998.

sponsors Elizabeth House, an emergency shelter for women and children who are victims of domestic abuse, poverty or abandonment.

The baptismal font in St. Charles Borromeo Church in Arlington. Situated near the entrance of the church, the font's placement serves as a reminder that baptism is the first of the Sacraments of Initiation.

BLESSED SACRAMENT

A celebration of First Holy Communion at Blessed Sacrament in Alexandria in 1994.

Serving parts of the City of Alexandria and South Arlington, Blessed Sacrament Parish has grown to include over 7,400 members since its foundation in 1945. For the first 42 years of its existence, parishioners worshipped in the school (a building originally planned for a school gym) and other less than ideal settings until the construction of the present church in 1988. The 58,000 square-foot structure makes a striking presence in a busy section of Alexandria. For many years the school was administered by the Sisters of the Holy Cross,

Blessed Sacrament Church in Alexandria.

but now the 370-student school is run by lay faculty and staff.

Blessed Sacrament stands as a good example of an active parish that stresses the need for its members to do the work of justice as they seek to live in the presence of the Lord. Toward this end, the parish's Social Concerns Committee works hard to encourage parishioners to become involved in various projects that provide aid to the poor and those living on the margins, both in Alexandria and in other parts of the world. In 1984, Blessed Sacrament Parish entered into a sister-parish relationship with St. Elizabeth of Hungary Parish in Elizabeth, West Virginia. When that parish became self sufficient, Blessed Sacrament began a sister-parish relationship with San Marcos in Gracias, Honduras. Through these partnerships, members of all these parishes learn from one another by sharing each other's "joys and sorrows, struggles and triumphs" as all strive to live up to their baptismal promises.

Spirituality is also important in the life of the community at Blessed Sacrament. To foster a personal relationship with Christ, the parish sponsors groups and activities such as the Legion of Mary, a monthly holy hour before the exposed Eucharist for mothers and their small children, a discussion group for Catholics who have recently returned to the practice of their faith and scripture faith-sharing groups. These are just a few examples of the way the priests and lay leaders attempt to deepen the faith of their brothers and sisters and create a greater sense of community at Blessed Sacrament.

GOOD SHEPHERD

Founded in 1965 shortly before the creation of the Diocese of Arlington, Good Shepherd Parish serves the Mount Vernon section of Alexandria. In the 1970s, the parish attained national attention over a dispute between the parish advisory board and Bishop Welsh. Unfortunately this led to deep division among the parishioners, but the passage of time has brought healing and Good Shepherd has moved on to become an active parish with much lay participation.

In 1984 the people of Good Shepherd dedicated a church building whose construction had been delayed as

The "Good Shepherd" tapestry in the narthex includes likenesses of clergy and laity, all of whom are under the all-encompassing protection of the Good Shepherd.

In 1984, Bishop Keating celebrated the liturgy of dedication of the new church.

a result of the problems of the 1970s. The structure can seat 800 and is of a good size for this 6,500-member parish community. For some time now the parish has had a vibrant ministry for Hispanics, whose numbers have been growing in recent years. Beginning in the early 1980s with a monthly Spanish Mass, over time this ministry has expanded. In the 1990s Good Shepherd began holding two Sunday liturgies in Spanish, which are attended by 1,000 people each weekend. In addition, the pastoral staff has grown to include a full-time Spanish-speaking priest, a Hispanic ministry coordinator and part-time Spanish-speaking catechetics and music directors. Both English-speaking and Spanish-speaking parishioners feel at home in Good Shepherd, and the pastoral staff works hard to forge unity among all the parish members.

Good Shepherd Church in Alexandria

QUEEN OF APOSTLES

Queen of Apostles Parish was founded in 1963 for Catholics in the northwest section of Alexandria. A moderate sized parish, today Queen of Apostles has about 3,000 members, and its school has an enrollment of 275 students. Originally staffed by Dominican Sisters, the school is now administered by laity. Notre Dame Hall, which once served as a convent, is now used by the Notre Dame Graduate School of Christendom College.

In the early 1990s the church underwent an interior renovation. Completed in September 1993, the refurbished sanctuary is made of Italian marble and includes an archway displaying gilded statues of the twelve apostles and Mary, Queen of the Apostles. During the renovations, daily Mass was held in the convent of the Poor Sisters of St. Joseph who have their regional house and novitiate nearby.

Queen of Apostles is a truly international parish with members from more than 30 nationalities spanning several socio-economic levels. Its stress on the beautiful celebration of the liturgy in which there is much lay participation helps to remind all who worship there of the unity and equality of all men and women.

Queen of Apostles Church in Alexandria.

Queen of Apostles parishioners participate in "Christmas in April," a program which rehabilitates housing for the poor.

Queen of Apostles' First Holy Communion Class, 1998.

ST. JOSEPH

The founding of the first African-American parish in Northern Virginia came largely thanks to the Josephite Fathers, a religious community founded in 1892 to minister to African Americans. In the early years of the twentieth century, Father Charles E. Hannigan, S.S.J., began making regular visits from his home in Richmond to a small group of black Catholics living in Alexandria. His regular ministrations soon helped to forge a unity among the black Catholics in Alexandria. Eventually with the help of Ms. Katie Bowman, Ms. Carrie Crouch, Mr. John Johnson and Mr. John Parker, Father Hannigan, obtained the support of Bishop Denis J. O'Connell of Richmond to start a separate parish for African-American Catholics in Alexandria. Although the bishop gave his approval, O'Connell left it up to these parish leaders to raise the funds to build a new church.

Since at this time most of Alexandria's black Catholics had low-paying jobs, raising the capital for a new church was not easy. However, the founders' hopes were greatly buoyed up when they received an $8,000 donation from Mother (now Saint) Katherine Drexel. A member of a wealthy family, the convert-foundress of the Sisters of the Blessed Sacrament, a religious community of women dedicated to evangelization among African-American and Native-American people, distributed much of her inheritance to advance apostolates directed toward these populations. Mother Drexel's contribution helped the founders of St. Joseph's to purchase property on the corner of North Columbus and Wythe Streets as the site for their church, which was dedicated on May 14, 1916.

Liturgy celebrating the 65th anniversary of the foundation of St. Joseph's.

St. Joseph Church, Alexandria

A bit earlier in 1916, the parish had begun operating a school in the church basement, and in 1931 a separate four-room school building was completed. The Oblate Sisters of Providence, a religious order founded for African-American women, agreed to administer the school. In order to teach here, the sisters had to commute by segregated buses from their convent in Southeast Washington, although parishioners would often drive them to and from school. The Oblate Sisters remained here until the school closed in 1969.

In 1967, St. Joseph's ceased to be a parish strictly for African Americans and received territorial boundaries. However, it continues to have a largely African-American congregation. Although with less than 500 registered parishioners it is considered small in comparison with other Northern Virginia parishes. It retains a vibrant spirit and remains true to its origins as a parish where black Catholic spirituality is both respected and celebrated.

ST. LAWRENCE

Founded in 1967, originally St. Lawrence was a country parish with just 400 families. As with many other parishes in Northern Virginia, first inside the Beltway and now beyond, St. Lawrence Parish has experienced tremendous growth. It now has over 8,300 registered parishioners. It is located in the Franconia section of Alexandria, close to Interstate 95 and the Springfield Mall.

Since development continues to bring new families with small children into the area, there has been discussion for some time about starting a parochial school at St. Lawrence. Until those plans come to fruition, some families send their children to schools attached to other nearby parishes, including St. Bernadette's in Springfield.

Begun by Father Franklyn M. McAfee, St. Lawrence's Prayer Garden is a quiet place to reflect on the beauty of God's creation.

Sanctuary of St. Lawrence.

Bell tower at St. Louis

ALEXANDRIA

ST. LOUIS

Situated near U.S. Route 1, St. Louis is a large parish and today has more than 8,400 parishioners. Its origins go back to the chapel of the Sacred Heart, which in 1925 was founded as a mission of St. Mary's in Alexandria. In 1949, the chapel was raised to the status of a parish and placed under the patronage of St. Louis.

The present St. Louis church was built in 1962, and thanks to the generosity of parishioners who raised more than $1.2 million dollars, it and several other parish buildings were renovated between 1988 and 1994. The school too received some needed repairs and improvements and today has an enrollment of 450 students.

For some time now the area along Route 1 has been one of the poorest sections of Fairfax County. Conscious of the needs of their neighbors, St. Louis parishioners have been involved in United Community Ministries (UCM), a network of churches that provide assistance to the needy of the city, especially in southern Alexandria. Over the years, this aid has taken various forms from providing emergency food and shelter to offering computer-training classes to those seeking employment. Whatever the type of assistance, St. Louis parishioners remain committed to following the teachings of Jesus which call for service to those in need.

Adoration of the Blessed Sacrament helps to remind worshippers that the celebration of the Eucharist is the central action of Catholics.

ST. MARY

The first and oldest Catholic parish in the Commonwealth of Virginia, St. Mary's was founded in 1795 with help from President George Washington. The site of the original church, where the present St. Mary's Cemetery is located, was technically outside the City of Alexandria since at that time the law forbade the construction of a Catholic church within city limits.

In 1810, Father Francis Neale, the founding pastor of St. Mary's, moved the church to its present location on South Royal Street to be closer to the center of town. In the 1830s, the original church was torn down and its bricks were used to construct the portico of the Alexandria Lyceum on Washington Street. After the partial restoration of the Society of Jesus in 1805, the parish was given over to the Jesuits and remained in their care until 1891. Eventually work began on the construction of a church at the parish's new site, and the first section was completed in 1826. Progress on the church continued throughout the nineteenth century with parishioners often performing some of the work as well as the design and planning.

On June 6, 1929, lightning struck the church steeple while a parish group was meeting in the church. Immediately the lightning ignited the church's electrical system. Soon thick black smoke began emanating from the roof, and before the night was over, every fire-fighting apparatus in the City of Alexandria was involved in containing the conflagration which caused $60,000 worth of damage, including the loss of the organ. The parishioners moved quickly to restore their church, which was completed by 1932.

Over its more than two hundred years, St. Mary's has sponsored several different schools, several of which were short-lived. The first attempt came in 1830 with the help

St. Mary's Church c. 1916.

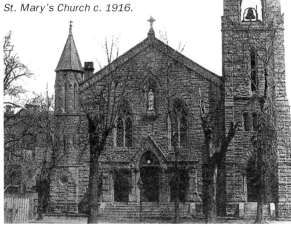

of the Sisters of Charity of Emmitsburg, Maryland, a community founded by Mother (now, Saint) Elizabeth Ann Seton. A group of her sisters started a school for girls in a house at the southwest corner of Fairfax and Duke Streets. The little venture flourished for a while, but for various reasons, the sisters withdrew in 1840 and the school closed. In 1833, a school for boys called "St. John's Academy" was opened by Jesuit Brother John Bridgon. Though the school grew quickly, attaining an enrollment of 64 by the end of its first year, it was forced to close in 1841 for financial reasons.

Holy Cross Sisters of St. Mary's School c. 1945. Front: Sisters Carolla, Conradine, Maritta, Marie Therese. Back: Sisters Jean LaSalle, Cyrpriana, Aquia, Beniti.

The first grade at St. Mary's School in the early 1920s with their teacher Sister Constantia, C.S.C. and Father Joseph Kelly.

It was not until after the Civil War that the parish was able to start a school that would last. In 1869, the Sisters of the Holy Cross came to St. Mary's and soon opened a free school, which is the direct ancestor of the present parish elementary school. They also operated "St. Mary's Academy," a private institution that charged tuition. Both schools thrived for many years, though the academy was eventually forced to close in 1990.

With the help of Father Denis O'Kane, S.J., St. Mary's pastor, in 1885 two Holy Cross sisters attempted to operate a school for African-American children. In many ways this was an incredible action given that at this time Alexandria was strictly segregated. Though it had a strong start, unfortunately enrollment eventually declined and the school closed in 1896.

As the "free" school continued to grow in the first decades of the twentieth century, in 1915 the Xaverian Brothers were brought in to run a separate school for boys for grades four through eight. Though popular during its brief life, the brothers' school was forced to close in 1934 because of the Depression. In the sunnier economic times after the Second World War, a large parochial school was opened in 1950 at a cost of $500,000. The new building had 12 classrooms, a library and a cafeteria.

By 1962, the school had reached its peak enrollment of 1,170, and then beginning in the 1970s, it began a steady decline to a low of 315 in the mid-1980s. Although it had to weather some difficult times, the school has remained viable and today educates 705 students.

Though St. Mary Parish is steeped in much history, in no way has it remained chained to the past. It is vibrant and active with over 11,000 registered parishioners. Located in the trendy and expensive Old Town section of Alexandria, the parish's eight Sunday Masses attract large crowds, including many young adults who live within walking distance. In addition, parishioners are involved in many activities, such as Meals on Wheels, the St. Camillus Group (a prayer and discussion forum for persons with serious illness) and several CYO groups for young people.

St. Mary's Church.

ST. RITA

Established as a mission of St. Mary's in Old Town in 1914, St. Rita's was made a separate parish in 1924. Our Lady of Lourdes Parish in Arlington was originally founded as a mission of St. Rita's in the 1940s. Celebrating its 25th anniversary, St. Rita's moved into a beautiful new church on Russell Road, built in a neo-Gothic style. The interior of the church is decorated in an Italian motif, with many unique statues and bas relief Stations of the Cross.

A moderate size parish, St. Rita's comprises 825 families. One third are original founding parishioners, one third are immigrants from Central America, and the remaining third are young families moving back into the metro area from outside the Beltway. Serving the pastoral needs of such a diverse group has been a hallmark of the clergy and staff of the parish. Founded in 1952, St. Rita's School has a current enrollment of 225 students. The original faculty and administration of the school was drawn from the

Interior of St. Rita.

Sisters of St. Joseph of Chestnut Hill, Pennsylvania, with four religious sisters still in residence. Currently, a lay principal and faculty teach school children drawn from the parish boundaries, as well as neighboring Crystal City, Pentagon City and Bolling Air Force Base. Graduates typically continue on to area parochial high schools and college preparatory schools.

St. Rita Church in Alexandria.

ANNANDALE

HOLY SPIRIT

Holy Spirit in Annandale.

Formed from parts of St. Michael's and St. Leo's parishes in 1964, Holy Spirit first held Masses and religious education classes in rented space at W.T. Woodson High School. However, the priests and parishioners soon set to work to construct a parish plant. By 1967, they had constructed both a school and a church, the latter of which won awards for its Oriental-style design. The inspiration for this came from Holy Spirit's founding pastor, Father Paul Cauwe, C.I.C.M., who previously had worked as a missionary in Asia. Originally Missionhurst priests served the parish, but eventually pastoral care was turned over to Arlington diocesan priests.

Since Holy Spirit is so large, with over 9,500 registered parishioners, the parish hums with activity. Some of its organizations include the women's council,

the men's club, the sharing committee, the bereavement committee, the youth group, the Cursillo community, the pro-life group and the Heart of Jesus prayer group. The Pre-K-to-8 school has an enrollment of 500 while the religious education program has over 800 students. To accommodate the needs of all these groups, the parish has had to enlarge its facilities. In 1987 a Pastoral Center was dedicated. It includes living space for the priests, rectory offices and meeting rooms. Three years later a gymnasium was built. It is now used extensively by both the school and parish groups.

Interior of Holy Spirit.

ST. AMBROSE

The youngest of the four parishes in Annandale, St. Ambrose was founded in 1966 when Northern Virginia was still part of the Richmond diocese. At its start, the parish had fewer than 1,000 parishioners. Today that number has risen to more than 2,800. For the first ten years of its existence, the parish priests celebrated Mass in rented space in a public school and later in a provisional church. The present church was not dedicated until December 1977. Because of some design defects, the building's cupola required extensive renovations in 1990. Soon after, the altar was moved to a central location and surrounded by pews on all sides in accord with the teaching of the Second Vatican Council that the altar should be of central focus during the liturgy.

In response to the need for more slots in Catholic schools, in 1995 the parish opened an elementary school with a beginning enrollment of 200. The founding principal, Mrs. Judith Lesniak, performed an incredible and unenviable task in putting together a school from scratch. Unfortunately, in December 1997, Mrs. Lesniak was killed in a car accident. Her untimely death was mourned by many who respected her for her deep faith and commitment to Catholic schools. The work she began has continued to flourish. Today St. Ambrose School has more than 230 students as well as a waiting list.

Mrs. Judith Lesniak, founding principal of St. Ambrose School, with students Patrick Hansen, Kristina Craun, Tony Accinelli, and Ashley Coles.

Bishop Thomas J. Welsh breaks ground for St. Ambrose Church on September 19, 1976.

ST. MICHAEL

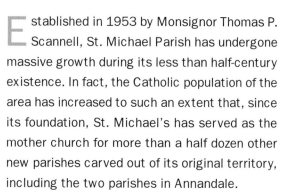

Established in 1953 by Monsignor Thomas P. Scannell, St. Michael Parish has undergone massive growth during its less than half-century existence. In fact, the Catholic population of the area has increased to such an extent that, since its foundation, St. Michael's has served as the mother church for more than a half dozen other new parishes carved out of its original territory, including the two parishes in Annandale.

Set on 45 acres, the parish complex includes a church, rectory, convent and two school buildings. With an enrollment of 500, St. Michael's School is one of the largest in the Arlington diocese. Since its opening, the school has been staffed by the Sisters, Servants of the Immaculate Heart of Mary (IHM) from Philadelphia. A large number of sisters still teach in the school. The parish also sponsors perpetual adoration of the Eucharist in a separate chapel which opened in 1984.

Left: Sanctuary of St. Michael's Church in Annandale. Bottom: This building, which also includes a recently refurbished gymnasium, houses grades K through 4 of St. Michael's School.

ST. THERESA

One of the youngest parishes in the diocese, St. Theresa was established in 1991 by Bishop Keating with Msgr. James W. McMurtrie as the founding pastor. At first, Mass was held in Broad Run High School and a local Protestant church. Then, in 1995, a school building was constructed, and its gym is now used for both Sunday and weekday liturgies. The parish offices are also located in the school. St. Theresa is located in Loudoun County, which continues to see much development since the recent opening of the Greenway toll road, a privately owned highway running parallel to Route 7. At the time of its establishment, the parish had fewer than 500 parishioners. Ten years later that number has reached 5,100.

St. Theresa opened a school in 1995 and graduated its first class of 16 eighth graders in June 1997. Popular since its opening, the school has an enrollment of 440 and a long waiting list. The parish will be out of debt by June 2002, and then can focus on the work of building a church.

St. Theresa School in Ashburn.

NATIVITY

Founded in 1977, Nativity Parish was established to serve the increasing number of Catholics drawn into central Fairfax County by ever increasing job opportunities. Today the parish has grown to more than 4,000 families which includes a large Hispanic population. The modern style church seats 1,000, and several weekend Masses fill the building, most notably the 11 a.m. liturgy when the youth choir attracts a standing room only congregation. This liturgical celebration is not the only place where young people make their presence known. The parish school has an enrollment of 250, and the Religious Education Program enrolls more than 1,600. Other youth involvement encompasses a vibrant youth group which reaches out to the poor, an active CYO program and scouting programs, for both boys and girls. In addition to these activities, Nativity supports a robust complement of activities for adults, which includes the Women of Nativity, Knights of Columbus chapter, craft groups and

The decorated sanctuary at Nativity during Christmas, 2000.

a "Mom and Me" group for young mothers and their toddlers. Programs for the spiritual development of the parishioners include RCIA, Legion of Mary, Bible Study, ministry to the newly married, Hispanic and Charismatic Prayer Groups, Cursillo and Our Lady of Knock Society. Pastoral Ministry involves Grief Support as well as ministry to the elderly, sick and the homebound. One of the hallmarks of the parish is its many outreach programs to the poor and needy, most notably its voluntary Lenten "Starfish" program which, over the past few years, has generated monies to build homes in the slums of Port au Prince, Haiti, along with medical help to this, the poorest country in the Western Hemisphere.

Nativity Parish in Burke.

ST. TIMOTHY CHURCH

In 1996 St. Timothy Church was enlarged and can now seat 1,400.

B egun in 1924 as a mission of St. Mary of Sorrows in Fairfax Station, today St. Timothy Church with almost 15,000 registered parishioners is one of the largest parishes in the diocese. By the time it was made an independent parish in 1969, the area around St. Timothy had begun to see residential development and an increase in the Catholic population. Thanks to both Dulles Airport and the many high-tech firms whose headquarters have sprung up along the Dulles Access Road, this growth has continued.

By the early 1990s the numbers celebrating Sunday Mass at St. Timothy had increased to such an extent that the 750-seat church was no longer adequate. In 1993, the parish launched a $4 million fund-raising campaign to enlarge the church and other parish facilities. The capital campaign was ultimately a success, and in 1996 the parish celebrated the opening of an expanded church which now seats 1,400 people. In addition, the school built a new cafeteria, gym and more classroom space. A new rectory was also added.

Development along the Dulles Corridor seems to know no end. To minister to the region's growing Catholic community, in 1999 Bishop Loverde announced the establishment of two new parishes in the Chantilly-Herndon area. Despite these additional churches, it seems that St. Timothy's will remain one of the larger parishes in the diocese with the opportunities and challenges so large a congregation offers.

St. Timothy Church in Chantilly.

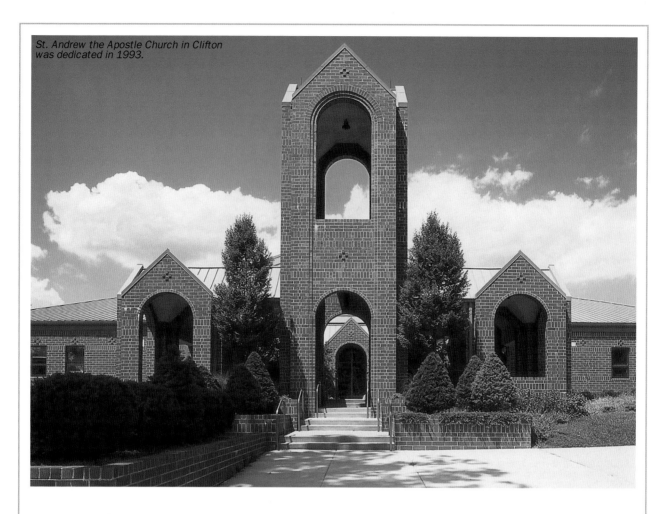

St. Andrew the Apostle Church in Clifton was dedicated in 1993.

CLIFTON-CENTREVILLE

ST. ANDREW THE APOSTLE

One of the newest and largest parishes in the diocese, St. Andrew the Apostle was founded by Bishop Keating in 1989 who carved it from the territory of St. Timothy Parish in Chantilly. For the first years of its existence, the parish celebrated Mass in Centreville High School, but Monsignor Hannan, the founding pastor, and the parishioners quickly set to work to construct the church that was dedicated in 1993. A school was also opened in that year. Today it has an enrollment of almost 300 students.

Situated in the westernmost part of Fairfax County, St. Andrew includes a large number of parishioners who work for the federal government at the Pentagon or for the Mobil Corporation. At its foundation, the parish had about 1,200 families. Thanks to the continued development of the area as well as a strong effort by members of the parish's chapter of the Legion of Mary who went door-to-door performing a parish census and inviting families to become involved in the new parish, the number of registered parishioners now exceeds 9,000. In an effort to meet the needs of the populous congregation, the parish supports many activities including several groups for young people.

Interior of St. Andrew the Apostle.

ST. CLARE OF ASSISI

Founded in 1980 as a mission of St. Timothy Parish, a new chapel was placed under the patronage of St. Clare to honor a group of Poor Clare nuns who had recently established a monastery in Alexandria. In 1989, St. Clare became a dependent mission of the newly established parish of St. Andrew the Apostle. As a result of the continued growth of the region, in August 1996 St. Clare was made an independent parish with Msgr. Frank E. Mahler as the founding pastor. Today it boasts about 1,700 parishioners.

St. Clare of Assisi Church in Clifton.

St. Anthony in King George is a mission of St. Elizabeth in Colonial Beach. The church was dedicated by Bishop Denis J. O'Connell of Richmond in 1917. The two-acre lot was purchased for $250 and it cost an additional $2,200 to construct the church building. It was enlarged to its present size in 1986.

COLONIAL BEACH

ST. ELIZABETH

The old St. Elizabeth Church was built in 1906.

St. Elizabeth, the only Catholic parish in Westmoreland County, was founded in 1906 and comprised an area larger than a thousand square miles for quite some time. For many years, priests from the Richmond diocese used to "ride the circuit" in horsedrawn buggies. These traveling priests visited mission stations, chapels, and Catholic families scattered extensively throughout the Northern Neck, a peninsula bordered by the Potomac River on the north and the Rappahannock River on the south.

In 1943, priests of the Missionary Servants of the Most Holy Trinity began serving St. Elizabeth Parish. They traveled and logged thousands of miles on their cars as they journeyed to celebrate Mass for their far-flung flock. These Trinitarian priests were replaced in 1993 by priests of the Arlington diocese. Although a new parish has been established for the southern part of the Northern Neck, thus ending extended journeys made by the priests, St. Elizabeth Parish still remains extremely large and comprises all of King George County and

St. Elizabeth Church, Colonial Beach.

the western portion of Westmoreland County. The eastern portion of Westmoreland County is serviced by St. Francis de Sales Catholic Church in Kilmarnock. Today, priests of the 1,300 member parish celebrate Mass at St. Elizabeth's and at St. Anthony Mission in King George. Parish priests also celebrated Mass at the Sacred Heart Chapel, Dahlgren, until 1998.

St. Elizabeth in Colonial Beach was originally built in 1906 and eventually became the mother church of the first parish developed in the Northern Neck. The new church building was dedicated on May 14, 1963, by the Most Reverend John Joyce Russell, Bishop of Richmond. The striking stained glass window over the main altar in the new church was transferred from the original church. The Stations of the Cross are by Stan Koshinski, an artist from Lynchburg. Both Sunday and weekday Masses are celebrated at St. Elizabeth. St. Anthony, the only Catholic church in King George County, was completed early in 1917. The spacious St. Anthony's hall, built in 1972, serves as classrooms for CCD classes and as a hall for meetings and church functions. Early in 1986, renovations and enlargement of the church were completed; later that same year during the summer, the church was dedicated by the Most Reverend John Richard Keating, Bishop of Arlington. Both Sunday and weekday Masses are celebrated at St. Anthony. In recent years, an increasing number of Spanish-speaking people have settled in the parish. St. Elizabeth has Mass in Spanish each Sunday for these parishioners.

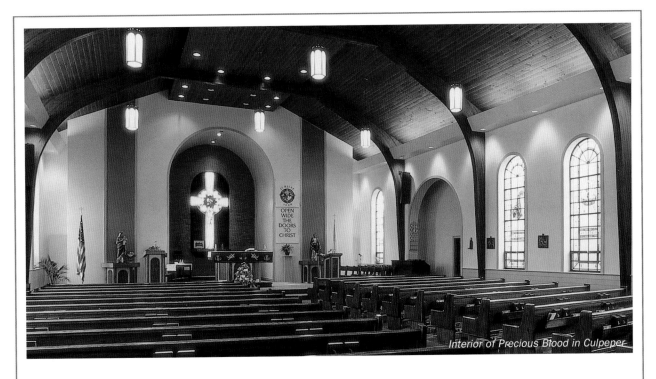

Interior of Precious Blood in Culpeper

CULPEPER

PRECIOUS BLOOD

In many ways Precious Blood Parish in Culpeper is located in mission territory since Catholics comprise less than four percent of the population which is heavily Southern Baptist. Founded in 1880 as a mission church, for many years Precious Blood was served by visiting priests until it became a regular parish founded in 1946 by Rev. Maurice du Castilion. At the invitation of Bishop Ireton, the Missionhurst Fathers took charge of the new parish, and this community continues to provide a priest for service here. On August 5, 1983, a new church was dedicated by Bishop Keating who had just been installed as the second Bishop of Arlington the day before. Though

a relatively small parish with fewer than 1,900 members, Precious Blood maintains a full complement of groups and activities.

In an effort to reach out to Catholics who live too far from Culpeper to worship here on a regular basis, in 1981 St. Peter Mission was established. St. Peter is the only Catholic church in Rappahanock County, which by any standard is small, having fewer than 10,000 full-time residents. For the first 11 years of its existence, Mass was held in a public school, but a church and a small rectory were eventually built in 1992. Since 1993, diocesan priests have served St. Peter Mission.

In 1983, Precious Blood began operating a pre-school program, which by the mid-1990s enrolled more than 70 students. Because of the success of the small school and the promise of more growth in the area, in 1997 the Arlington diocese opened Epiphany School. The new venture has proved to be a success, and the school, which includes grades pre-K through 5, today has an enrollment of 150 pupils.

At a celebration of Precious Blood's golden jubilee, those who have been parishioners since 1946 were honored for their long-time commitment and involvement in the parish. Seated: Miss Edwina Carley, Mr. Joseph Trolio, Mrs. Edith Ouellette, Mr. Emilien Ouellette. Standing: Mrs. Magdalene Mooney, Mrs. Bea Gulas, Mr. L.A. Roades, Father Leo Zonneveld, C.I.C.M., Mrs. Anna Marie Stringfellow, Father Joseph Lapauw, C.I.C.M., Mrs. Hazel Veduce, Mr. Sam Veduce.

HOLY FAMILY

Established in September 1970, Holy Family is located in the southeastern area of Prince William County. The parish church was built in 1974, after having celebrated Masses in local public schools for the parish's first few years. In 1990, an activities hall was added that includes 18 classrooms, a gym and a kitchen. After opening these new facilities, Holy Family began a pre-school program. In 1997, the process of expansion into a complete elementary school was begun with the opening of a first grade. At present Holy Family School has an enrollment of 160 students in grades pre-K through four. The parish's CCD program is one of the largest in the diocese, having more one 1,000 students.

Holy Family is a young parish. Its 7,100 parishioners include many families with small children. To encourage and support this large segment of the parish, Holy Family sponsors a Young Adults group, a Family Life group and a summer Bible school for children.

Holy Family, Dale City

Sanctuary of Holy Family Church in Dale City.

ST. LEO THE GREAT

For more than forty years, St. Leo the Great Catholic Church has served the Catholic residents of the City of Fairfax and surrounding neighborhoods as a witness to the Good News of Jesus Christ. St. Leo's plays a pivotal role in the quality of life found in Fairfax, and in the Diocese of Arlington as a leading parish community.

The parish was founded in 1957 as a mission of St. Mary of Sorrows, Fairfax Station, with 450 families. The present church was completed in 1965 and the school building has undergone two expansions, the most recent in 1991 with the addition of classrooms, library and gymnasium. The original church was renovated in 1998 to become a center for parish meetings and adult education programs.

Today, there are nearly 3,000 households representing nearly 10,000 souls. Alongside the priests and staff, there are more than 60 parish groups, continuing education opportunities, prayer groups and countless activities for fellowship and service throughout the year.

Interior of St Leo the Great in Faifax.

Nearly 600 children are enrolled in the parish school, whose excellence has continued to make it a leader among Catholic schools. Another 600 children are enrolled in parish religious education programs, both in English and Spanish. More than 4,000 needy people are served annually by a dynamic parish chapter of the St. Vincent de Paul Society and other outreach programs such as the Ambassadors of St. Camillus, a group of laity active in ministry to the sick and elderly in local nursing homes, and Knights of Columbus Father Diamond Council. St. Leo's is also involved in Hispanic ministry, providing Mass and sacraments in Spanish for the City of Fairfax as well as surrounding parishes which do not offer ministry in Spanish.

St. Leo the Great looks forward to a bright future of continued growth, continuing to respond to God's call-both to Himself, and to one another.

St. Leo Church in Fairfax.

ST. MARY OF SORROWS

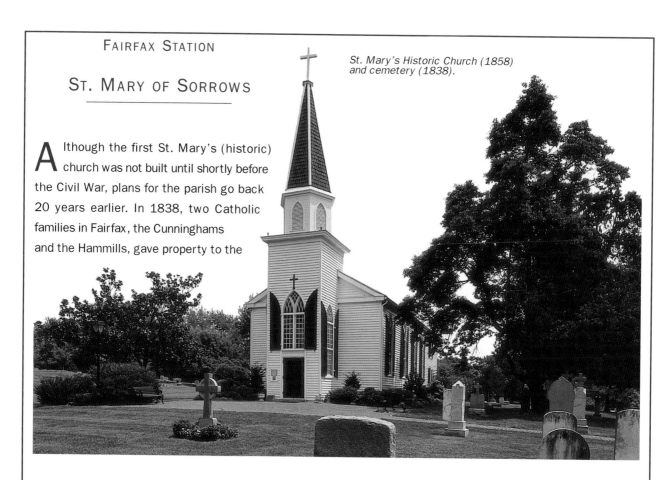

St. Mary's Historic Church (1858) and cemetery (1838).

Although the first St. Mary's (historic) church was not built until shortly before the Civil War, plans for the parish go back 20 years earlier. In 1838, two Catholic families in Fairfax, the Cunninghams and the Hammills, gave property to the Diocese of Richmond in hope of gaining a church and a priest. In the late 1850s, construction finally began, and on September 19, 1858, Bishop John McGill presided at the laying of the cornerstone. When completed, St. Mary, the first Catholic church in Fairfax County, was made a mission of St. Mary's in Alexandria. The newly constructed church was soon filled each Sunday with Irish laborers who had come to the area to work on the construction of the Orange and Alexandria Railroad.

St. Mary's remained a dependent mission of St. Mary's and later of St. James in Falls Church until 1918 when it was made an independent parish. The next year an old house was bought, refurbished and made the parish rectory for the parish's first pastor, Father Valentine D. Cuevas, an émigré priest from Mexico. Both Father Cuevas and his successors celebrated the Eucharist in other parts of the county and set up permanent missions in Centreville, Manassas, Pleasant Valley, Haymarket and Gainsville. By the 1950s, the parish had bought property in Annandale and established a mission which eventually became St. Michael Parish.

In the mid-1960s, Bishop John Russell of Richmond invited the Claretian Fathers to staff the parish, and members of the community served here for almost 30 years until their departure in 1990. Under the leadership of the Claretians, the parish built a new, larger church building to accommodate the growing number of families joining St. Mary. The 800-seat church was dedicated on December 15, 1989. Today both Sunday and weekday Masses are celebrated in both the historic and the new churches for this 3,700-family parish.

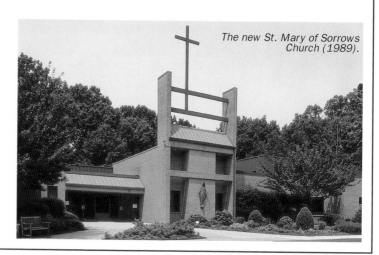

The new St. Mary of Sorrows Church (1989).

ST. PAUL CHUNG

As in other parts of the U.S., the size of the Asian-American population has been increasing at a fast pace in recent years. This has been especially true for the Korean Catholic population of Northern Virginia, which received its own parish in 1996 with the establishment of St. Paul Chung. Beginning in the mid-1980s this small but growing community would meet in several other parishes, and a Korean priest would celebrate the Sunday Mass in Korean. With the establishment of the parish and the construction of the present church and rectory in 1995, the members of this vibrant community are able to come together regularly to reaffirm their Catholic faith and celebrate their common heritage.

On an average Sunday, Korean-American families travel from all over Northern Virginia to gather for the liturgy in their native tongue. The parish conducts a religious education program for more than 500 children using texts in both Korean and English. With the promise of more growth, the parish is making preliminary plans to construct a youth center for the many teens and young adults who form so important a part of the parish community.

Above: Several times each year parishioners come to Mass in traditional Korean dress proudly recalling their heritage. Below: St. Paul Chung Church in Fairfax.

ST. RAYMOND OF PENAFORT

Since its establishment in the Fall of 1996, St. Raymond of Penafort Parish became the sixty-third parish in the Diocese of Arlington. The diocese purchased a home at 8900 Triple Ridge Road. Soon afterwards, the St. Raymond parish family was celebrating daily Masses in the basement of the new rectory. The founding pastor, Father Salvator L. Ciullo, remained in this post until the summer of 2000, when Father James R. Gould, former diocesan Director of Vocations, replaced him as the new pastor.

With ever increasing attendance, the parish soon needed a larger space and began gathering for Mass at the West Springfield High School auditorium on weekends and at Christ United Methodist Church for the daily Masses. Presently, the Springfield Volunteer Fire Department otherwise known as the "Holy Fire Hall" on Backlick Road serves as a church for weekend Masses, while daily Mass is offered at Angelus Academy, a local private Catholic elementary school.

Currently St. Raymond of Penafort parish numbers over 650 registered families. Judging by the decibels emanating from the parish munchkins, and future choir members, visitors get the warm impression that the average age in the parish is thirteen and that the projected cry room for St. Raymond's will fill one, or both, transepts of the new church.

With the county's approval for a new church that will seat 850 people, the St. Raymond parish family is looking forward to a ground-breaking ceremony in June of 2002. The new parish site is on Pohick Road, adjacent to the Fairfax County Parkway. Plans for the new church include space for a parish hall, library, and eight classrooms. A new rectory behind the church will house additional parish offices.

ST. ANTHONY

Established in 1921 as a mission station of St. Mary's in Alexandria, St. Anthony was eventually transferred to the care of two other area parishes before it was made an independent parish in 1952 and given to the care of priests of the Society of the Precious Blood. From

Corpus Christi school in Falls Church.

1952 to 1954, to accommodate the ever-growing congregation, Mass was held in the Culmore Shopping Center in what is now Tony's Place. A small wooden building that had served as the original chapel is now Holy Cross Romanian Orthodox Church on Leesburg Pike. After the construction of the school building in 1954, Mass was celebrated in the school gym and the parish community continued to meet here for liturgy until the present church was dedicated in March 1970.

The Sisters of the Precious Blood both founded and administered the school for many years until their departure in the 1980s. Because of falling enrollments, in 1989 St. Anthony School and St. Philip School, also in Falls Church, combined and were

renamed Corpus Christi School. This amalgamation has proven to be a success. Today Corpus Christi has more than 470 boys and girls enrolled in grades pre-K through eight.

The year 1989 brought other changes to St. Anthony. After more than 35 years of service, the Precious Blood Fathers announced that they would be withdrawing from the parish. Since their departure the parish has been served by the diocesan priests of Arlington.

A large parish with more than 8,000 members, St. Anthony also has a growing Hispanic population. To make these newcomers welcome, St. Anthony offers two Sunday liturgies in Spanish. In addition, for more than 20 years the Servants of St. Joseph, a group of religious sisters headquartered in Spain who have a convent nearby, have taught religious education and conducted home visitations.

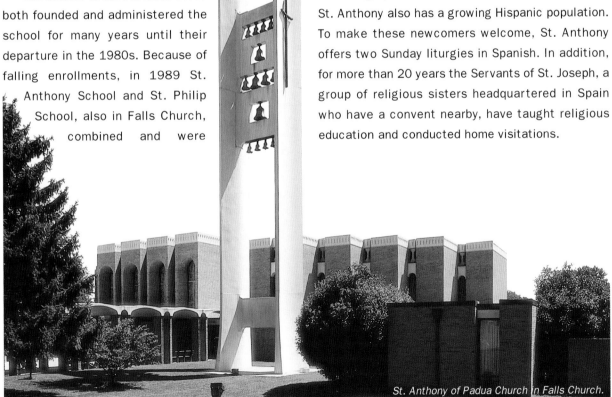

St. Anthony of Padua Church in Falls Church.

ST. JAMES

S hortly after the Civil War in 1873, St. James was established as a mission of St. Mary Parish in Alexandria. By the time it was raised to the status of a parish in 1892, St. James had only 325 parishioners. By 2001 that number had climbed to over 7,500. The present church was constructed in 1902 and was expanded in the early 1950s to meet the needs of a growing parish.

The parish opened a school in 1907 which continues to flourish to this day. Originally the Sisters of Perpetual Adoration staffed the school, but after their withdrawal in 1923, they were replaced by the Sisters, Servants of the Immaculate Heart of Mary who now mark more than 75 years of service to the community. One of the largest schools in the diocese with more than 660 students, in 1998 St. James School was named a Blue Ribbon School by the U.S. Department of Education in recognition of its academic excellence, parental involvement and community support.

In addition to this prestigious honor, other good things have been happening at St. James. In January 1999, a new $1.6 million gymnasium was opened representing

St. James Church in Falls Church.

the first major addition to the school campus in 30 years. Named in honor of an alumnus, Joseph B. Knecht, who became a life-long parishioner and the victim of an accident in 1997, the new facility is used for CYO basketball games, school fairs and other parish activities.

St. James conducts one of the largest schools in the Arlington diocese.

ST. PHILIP

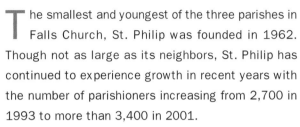

The smallest and youngest of the three parishes in Falls Church, St. Philip was founded in 1962. Though not as large as its neighbors, St. Philip has continued to experience growth in recent years with the number of parishioners increasing from 2,700 in 1993 to more than 3,400 in 2001.

During the mid-1980s, the parish suffered through some difficult financial times because of a growing deficit in the school. To keep Catholic education viable in the Falls Church area, in 1989 the school was combined with St. Anthony School to create Corpus Christi School. While grades one through eight are located at St. Anthony, the pre-school and kindergarten are housed in the former St. Philip School. The enrollment for these grades has reached 182 students.

In 1967, Father John T. Cilinski, second pastor of St. Philip's, led the ground breaking for the second phase of construction of the parish facilities.

St. Philip Church in Falls Church.

ST. MARY

One of the oldest parishes in Northern Virginia, St. Mary was founded in 1858 under the title "St. Mary of the Immaculate Conception." The original church, completed in 1859, was used by the Union Army as a makeshift hospital and a stable. In 1871, the parish received its first resident pastor with the appointment of Father Hugh J. McKeefrey. Although the new priest had a congregation of fewer than 300, he had responsibility for missions

The first St. Mary Church in Fredericksburg was completed in 1859.

in Ashland, Chesterfield, King George and Tappahannock, which surely kept him busy in caring for the scattered Catholics in these far-flung locations. By modern standards St. Mary took in a huge territory. Since the time of Father McKeefrey's administration, five new parishes have been carved from the original boundaries of St. Mary.

Between the end of the Civil War and the end of the Second World War, the Catholic community of Fredericksburg saw little expansion, increasing to only

350 by 1946. However, the postwar era brought strong and steady growth, and by 1958 St. Mary had reached 1,200 parishioners. This increase in the Catholic population soon led to the need for a larger church, which was dedicated in 1971.

Although St. Mary has never had its own parochial school, in 1948 at the invitation of the pastor, the Daughters of Wisdom established Montfort Academy as an elementary school for Catholic children of Fredericksburg. The school remained in operation until June 1998 when the sisters were forced to close the institution citing a lack of vocations. Fortunately that fall, the diocese opened Holy Cross Academy, a new inter-parish elementary school. Staffed by the Oblate Sisters of St. Francis de Sales and lay teachers, Holy Cross has proven to be a success, now enrolling 502 students.

Although several other parishes have originated from St. Mary, it nevertheless has remained geographically large encompassing the city of Fredericksburg and a part of neighboring Spotsylvania County and Stafford County. The parish supports a variety of activities for more than 10,000 registered parishioners.

Sanctuary of the present St. Mary Church.

In April 2000, Father Philip S. Majka, pastor of St. Patrick, celebrated the thirtieth anniversary of his ordination.

FREDERICKSBURG (CHANCELLORSVILLE)

ST. PATRICK

An offshoot of St. Mary in Fredericksburg, St. Patrick was founded in 1983 taking in most of Spotsylvania County. Msgr. R. Roy Cosby was the founding pastor. Since its beginning the new parish has experienced rapid growth and today has more than 5,200 parishioners. In 1985, the present church was built on the site of the Civil War battle of Chancellorsville, fought in May 1863. The rectory is located about twenty minutes from the church. A few years after the construction of the church, St. Matthew Chapel was built next to the rectory in a style similar to St. Patrick church.

Because St. Patrick is the only Catholic parish in Spotsylvania County, many parishioners must travel far to participate in Sunday Mass and other parish activities. For some time the parish has maintained its own small fleet of vans and buses to transport the hundreds of children in the CCD program from their public schools and to their homes after class.

In the fall of 1990, the parish opened St. Patrick School with an initial enrollment of seven kindergartners. A new grade was added each year, and in 1998 the school graduated its first class of eighth-graders. The school has now reached an enrollment of 208.

St. Patrick Church in Spotsylvania County.

ST. JOHN THE BAPTIST

Although St. John the Baptist was not established as a regular parish until 1940, the Catholic community of Front Royal was organized much earlier. In 1884, Bishop Keane of Richmond dedicated the church which is still used today. The plan to build a Catholic church in the town goes back to the time of the Civil War when the Jenkins family of Baltimore, MD desired to erect a church in memory of their 27-year-old son who died of typhoid fever while a Confederate soldier. (During the Civil War more soldiers died of disease than from injuries sustained from battle.) Originally the Jenkins family wanted to build a church in Warm Springs, where their son died, but were eventually convinced to erect it in Front Royal since it had a larger Catholic population. While the Jenkins family donated money for the church building, altar, pews, vestments and the vessels used for Mass, the Macatee family gave the land on which the church was built.

For more than a century the historic church, which could seat 140, was suitable for the size of the parish, but by the 1990s St. John began to experience sustained growth brought about by an increase in the number of families with weekend houses in the area. In June 1997, the parish began building a new 450-seat church, which was dedicated on the feast of St. John the Baptist in 1998. The only Catholic parish in Warren County, St. John the Baptist includes the western part of Fauquier County and has almost 1,100 parishioners.

Top: St. John the Baptist Parish's original church was built in 1884 (right) at a cost of $5,500. In 1998, a larger church (left) was constructed next to the old one to accommodate a growing congregation.
Middle: Interior of the historic church.
Bottom: A Sunday liturgy in the new church.

ST. MARK

Located in the southwestern portion of the diocese, St. Mark has the distinction of being the smallest parish in Arlington with just 100 parishioners. Originating in 1884 as a mission of St. John the Evangelist in Warrenton, it eventually passed under the administration of Holy Comforter in Charlottesville, Precious Blood in Culpeper and St. John in Orange before it was made an independent parish in 1964. As members of a parish quite conscious of its history, parishioners still worship in the original church building, which was constructed in 1884.

For many years Missionhurst priests served at St. Mark, but recently priests of the Arlington diocese have assumed administration of the parish. At present St. Mark does not have a resident priest. The pastor of St. John in Orange serves as administrator. Pastoral ministry at St. Mark can present challenges for any priest. The part of Orange County in which the parish is located has suffered from a stagnant economy for decades. As a result, many who were reared in the area are forced to move elsewhere in search of work, and in recent years the parish has lost a sizeable number of parishioners. Despite its small size, the parish has a long tradition of people volunteering their time to work around the church and do repairs. The challenge for the future is to encourage greater participation in liturgical ministries as well as continued outreach to inactive Catholics and the unchurched of the area.

St. Mark Church in Gordonsville.

GREAT FALLS

ST. CATHERINE OF SIENA

"The Great Falls Catholic Community" came to birth as a mission of St. Luke, McLean, in 1968 through a petition from a family living in Great Falls. This family asked Fr. Pereira, then pastor of St. Luke, to start a mission in their town because they found the weekly commute to St. Luke for their children's religious education classes to be arduous. They were told that it would be established if they could secure the support of 110 people. The required number was soon found. Eleven years later, in June of 1979, St. Catherine of Siena was formally

established as a parish. Father Anthony Justs was the founding pastor. The present church was dedicated on October 8, 1981.

From a beginning of 100 plus people in 1968, thirty-three years later, St. Catherine of Siena has grown to include almost 4,000 members. To meet the needs of the growing congregation, in 1999 the parish broke ground for a new education center. To be completed in 2002, the new $3.6 million facility will include classrooms and a large social hall.

Recently, *Time magazine* featured St. Catherine of Siena Church as an example of a Catholic parish that reintroduced the use of Latin in the liturgy as well as other practices which previously had fallen into disuse amongst the overwhelming majority of American Catholics since the Second Vatican Council. With this return to traditional ways, as well as preaching which stresses unswerving obedience to the pope, St. Catherine of Siena attracts worshipers from beyond its boundaries who are seeking a more traditional practice of the Catholic faith.

Middle: In 1980, St. Catherine of Siena Parish, Great Falls, celebrated the groundbreaking for the present church. Left: Bishop Anthony Justs (second from right at a recent liturgy) was the founding pastor of St. Catherine of Siena Parish in 1979. Formerly an Arlington priest, in 1996 he was installed as the first Bishop of Jelgava in Latvia.

ST. JOSEPH

S ituated in the extreme northwestern part of Fairfax County, St. Joseph was founded in 1923 as a mission of St. James in Falls Church. In 1925, a small stone church was built for the congregation of 80, and in 1950, St. Joseph was made a regular parish. However, the parish did not receive a resident pastor until 1950 when the Holy Ghost Fathers agreed to take the parish.

In 1965, a new church and four classrooms were constructed to accommodate the growing parish. In fact, the growth of St. Joseph was so rapid that during the 1970s two new parishes, Christ the Redeemer in Sterling and St. Thomas à Becket in Reston, were carved out of St. Joseph's original territory. In 1981, the Holy Ghost Fathers who had served here for more than 30 years departed. They were immediately replaced by the Third Order Regular Franciscans who accepted charge of the parish at the invitation of Bishop Welsh. Also in the same year the parish

The new St. Joseph Church, constructed in 1994.

constructed a new hall to be used during the week as a cafeteria by the school and on the weekends as another site for liturgies since the church could not handle the growing crowds at Sunday Mass.

The Franciscans were not at St. Joseph long before the parish began making plans for a new church. On March 19, 1987, the feast of St. Joseph, a new 1,000-seat church was dedicated by Bishop Keating. The parish is presently in the process of expanding the parish hall to construct the parish office wing as well as add several meeting rooms. The school also has continued to grow and now has an enrollment of almost 600 students.

St. Joseph Church in Herndon.

HERNDON

ST. VERONICA

On June 17, 1999, Bishop Loverde announced the establishment of St. Veronica Parish in the Dulles Airport corridor. The diocese plans to locate the church at the intersection of Barnsfield and Centreville Roads between Chantilly and Herndon. It is hoped that St. Veronica's facilities will ease the overcrowding in the neighboring churches in Herndon, Chantilly and Reston which are also rapidly growing.

Since its establishment two years ago, St. Veronica has celebrated Mass in several locations, including a local elementary school and two Methodist churches, both in Herndon. The 1600-member parish is already busy raising funds for the construction of a church, a parish hall and possibly even a school.

The Oak Hill Elementary School cafeteria was the site of St. Veronica's Christmas liturgies in December 2000.
St. Veronica's parishioners get settled before Sunday Mass.

KILMARNOCK

ST. FRANCIS DE SALES

In terms of geographic area, St. Francis de Sales is one of the largest parishes in the diocese, covering Northumberland, Lancaster and Richmond Counties and the eastern part of Westmoreland County. However, in terms of number of parishioners it is one of the smallest with a little more than one thousand registered members. When the first church was built in 1885, it had the distinction of being the first Catholic church in the Northern Neck of Virginia. Before its construction, for thirty years priests from Fredericksburg came by steamship to celebrate Mass at the mission. Eventually priest members of the Missionary Servants of the Most Holy Trinity served St. Francis de Sales, which was raised to the status of a parish in 1966. In 1981, the Missionary Servants withdrew from the parish to be replaced by priests of the Arlington diocese. The parish also maintains St. Paul Mission in Hague at which one liturgy is celebrated every Sunday.

Unlike the many parishes in the northern part of the diocese which are filled with young families, parishioners at St. Francis de Sales tend to be older reflecting the demographics of the region. However, the parish has experienced steady growth in recent years because of the influx of retired persons relocating in the region, which remains one of the few undeveloped areas on the Mid-Atlantic coast.

Each Sunday parishioners of St. Francis de Sales fill their small brick church, which was built in 1956.

Sanctuary of St. Francis de Sales Church.

On September 8, 1999, the parish celebrated the dedication of the Our Lady of Fatima Prayer Garden. The new addition came thanks to the hard work of the St. Teresa of Avila Ladies Auxiliary and Infant Jesus of Prague Council of the Knights of Columbus. Left to right: Arthur T. Carroll Sr., Maxine Luxton, Arthur T. Booker Sr., Father James Bruse, Ernest Charlie, Bob Bannach, Paul Carren, Carol Kaptain, Fred Luxton, Mo Martin, Lou Carren and Steve Gerloff.

ST. ELIZABETH ANN SETON

One of the newest parishes in Prince William County, St. Elizabeth Ann Seton was founded in 1975 by Rev. Philip S. Majka, presently pastor of St. Patrick's Church, Fredericksburg, VA, and is also one of the largest in the diocese with more than 9,000 parishioners. Located close to Interstate 95, the area has experienced much development since the 1960s. The burgeoning growth has attracted many young families to the parish, bringing the average age of the parishioners to below forty.

In the early years Mass was offered in Rockledge Elementary School with seating provided on metal folding chairs. On special occasions, the congregation rented St. Matthew's Lutheran Church nearby. In 1981, a two-level interim church and Activities Center opened, and 1988 brought a new rectory. Although the interim church fulfilled its purpose, from its

In January 2000, parishioners from St. Elizabeth Ann Seton in Lake Ridge attended the annual Pro-Life March in Washington, D.C.

conception it was meant to be only temporary. By 1988 discussions of a new church building were underway. Ground was broken for the new structure in March 1993, and by May construction was in full swing. On August 28, 1994, Bishop Keating presided over the dedication of the $3.6 million new church. The new structure can seat 1,200, double the capacity of the old church, now used as a parish hall.

St. Elizabeth Ann Seton Church in Lake Ridge.

ST. JOHN THE APOSTLE

One of the oldest church buildings still in use in the diocese, St. John the Apostle in Leesburg was dedicated in 1878 by Bishop John J. Keane of Richmond. At the time of its foundation, the church was yet unnamed and was a mission of St. Peter's in Harper's Ferry, West Virginia.

Shortly after its founding, the new church became known by a series of names including Immaculate Conception, Mary of the Immaculate Conception, St. Mary's and Our Lady of Lourdes. In 1892, the many-named mission was canonically transferred to St. James in Falls Church and remained dependent on this parish until 1926. The following year it was renamed St. John the Apostle, an appellation the church has kept to the present. At the time of its creation as a separate parish, St. John was given dependent missions in Purcellville and Herndon. Both churches are now parishes in their own right. In 1947, the parish started a mission in Middleburg, which eventually became independent in 1975.

Under the leadership of Father Albert F. Pereira who became pastor in 1957, St. John made history in being the first parish in the United States to use the "Dialogue Mass." Developed before the Second Vatican Council, this form of the liturgy allowed for a fuller participation by the congregation, which had previously played a passive role at Mass. In more recent years the parish has experienced strong growth as the suburbs of Washington, D.C. push

Above: St. John's Church, which dates to 1878, is now known as the "Little Church."
Top left: St. John the Apostle, Leesburg, ca. 1883. At that time the mission church was known by several different names.

farther and farther west. To meet the needs of the growing congregation, St. John opened a parish center in 1992. The new facility contains eight classrooms, the parish offices and a large multi-purpose room, now accommodating four liturgies every Sunday, and one on Saturday. The added space was greatly needed by St. John's which now has 4,800 registered parishioners.

The parish center was constructed in 1992.

Top: Our Lady of the Valley rectory. Above: Interior of the church.

was still grumbling by anti-Catholic voices. Situated in a valley of the Shenandoah and Massanutten Mountains, the parish encompasses more than 300 square miles. In 1968, diocesan priests replaced the Redemptorist Fathers who had staffed it from the beginning. Since 1992 two different Third Order Regular Franciscans have served the parish, which has fewer than 500 parishioners.

Page County has traditionally been Lutheran with almost no native Catholic population. Today the parishioner base is comprised largely of resettled retirees and a number of converts. Though small, Our Lady of the Valley is alive and active. For some years parishioners have participated in Page One, an ecumenical charitable organization that provides food and clothing to Page County residents in need. Every summer, mothers in the parish conduct a Vacation Bible School for children aged three to nine. Also during the summer months, with the arrival of vacationers visiting nearby Luray Caverns and Skyline Drive, the parish experiences an increase in Sunday Mass participation.

LURAY

OUR LADY OF THE VALLEY

At the time of the establishment of Our Lady of the Valley in 1954, the Richmond diocese found it impossible to buy land for a church within the town of Luray. No resident was willing to sell property for a Catholic church. Finally, Bishop Ireton was able to arrange for the purchase of land outside the town limits, though there

Our Lady of the Valley, Luray, is the only Catholic parish in Page County.

Above: The parish's manicured landscape provides a bucolic setting for an outdoor Stations of the Cross.
Bottom: On June 14, 1992, Bishop Keating presided over the dedication of the new church.

MADISON

OUR LADY OF THE BLUE RIDGE

Serving all of Madison County in the southwestern corner of the diocese, Our Lady of the Blue Ridge parish was founded in 1974 as a mission of St. John in Orange.

Only three years later it became an independent parish. For the first few years the parish celebrated Eucharistic liturgies in a multi-purpose room of the local firehouse. In 1979, the parish built a rectory and chapel, and in 1992, a new church on Route 29 alongside the Seminole Trail.

Since Madison County is overwhelmingly rural, the parish has only 410 parishioners. Few parishioners are native to the area, many having arrived from other parts of the country. Though the Catholics of the county remain a minority, comprising less than three percent of the population, Our Lady of the Blue Ridge has worked hard to build up relationships with other Christian congregations. For example, at the dedication of the new church, a local non-denominational chorus sang during the Sunday liturgy, and later the same day, the parish held an ecumenical prayer service again to celebrate the dedication. The parish is an active participant in Madison Emergency Relief Association, a charitable organization that provides food, clothing, housing and employment assistance to those in need. During Lent, the parish participates in an inter-congregational Scripture study group, and parishioners also take part in several other annual activities that bring together people of different denominations.

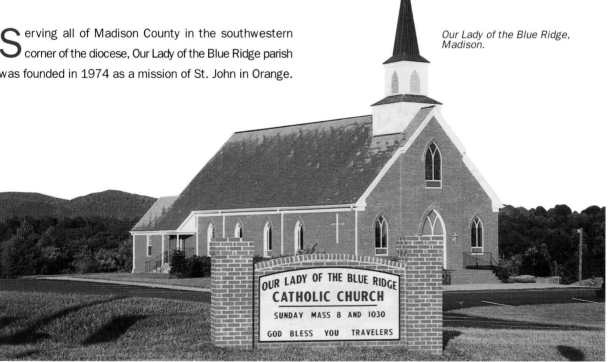

Our Lady of the Blue Ridge, Madison.

MANASSAS

ALL SAINTS

W hen All Saints was founded in 1878, the small mission church, which sat fewer than 100 parishioners, served hundreds of square miles with its jurisdiction extending north to the Potomac River, east to Woodbridge and Triangle, and west to the Bull Run Mountains. For many years priests would travel from Warrentown to celebrate Sunday Mass. In 1929, when All Saints was raised to the status of a parish, Father Michael Cannon became its first resident priest and pastor. From 1942 to 1993, Stigmatine priests took on the pastoral care of the parish. At their departure, Arlington diocesan priests replaced them.

In 1960, the parish opened All Saints School, which for many years was served by the Benedictine Sisters of Bristow, Virginia. To meet the needs of a growing enrollment, in 1985 a new addition housed a library, two classrooms and a multi-purpose room. In 1999,

the building was further expanded by a two-story wing that provided a computer lab, a resource room, science labs and several new classrooms, all of which comfortably accommodate the school's current 520 students.

With more than 18,000 registered parishioners, today All Saints claims the distinction of being the largest parish in Virginia. While the present church, built in 1974, seats 860, in recent years it has proven inadequate for the crowds that come to Mass each weekend. In 1995, All Saints launched a Building Fund Campaign to raise money toward the day when a larger church can be built. Until then, the parish makes do with the present facilities, but must offer nine weekend liturgies to avoid overcrowding. Also in recent years the parish has experienced growth in its Hispanic community. To meet the needs of these newcomers, All Saints has added two Sunday Masses in Spanish, and celebrates the cultural diversity of the community with love and faith.

Top left: In 1998, the parish celebrated Easter Sunday Mass in the Nissan Pavilion in nearby Bristow. In addition to the large number of catechumens and candidates received into the Church at the previous night's Easter Vigil, a number of infants were baptized at the concert stadium.
Top right: Interior of church.
Below: All Saints, Manassas.

SACRED HEART

The old Sacred Heart church was built in 1936.

Started in 1936 as a mission chapel, Sacred Heart was made an independent parish in 1984 and today has more than 3,500 registered parishioners. For many years the original wooden chapel was sufficient for the community's needs, but the growth that has come to the region in recent years necessitated the construction of a new church. It was dedicated in 1994. The larger structure can seat 500 persons and includes a daily Mass chapel, classrooms, offices, an elevator to make the facility handicapped-accessible and a social hall, which is located below the church.

An active parish, Sacred Heart supports many groups and activities for parishioners, including Sacred Heart-Area Senior Citizens (an interfaith seniors group), a Knights of Columbus council, and a social ministry committee.

Sacred Heart, Manassas, dedicated a new church in 1994.

St. John

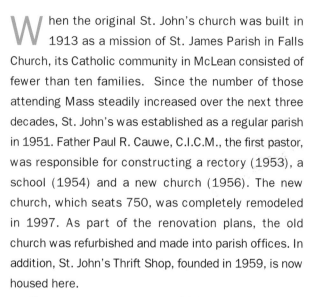

When the original St. John's church was built in 1913 as a mission of St. James Parish in Falls Church, its Catholic community in McLean consisted of fewer than ten families. Since the number of those attending Mass steadily increased over the next three decades, St. John's was established as a regular parish in 1951. Father Paul R. Cauwe, C.I.C.M., the first pastor, was responsible for constructing a rectory (1953), a school (1954) and a new church (1956). The new church, which seats 750, was completely remodeled in 1997. As part of the renovation plans, the old church was refurbished and made into parish offices. In addition, St. John's Thrift Shop, founded in 1959, is now housed here.

For many years and until 1993, St. John's School was staffed by the Sisters of Notre Dame of Chardon, Ohio. Today the school has an enrollment of 225 students who are served by a lay principal and faculty.

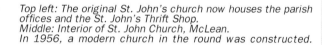

Top left: The original St. John's church now houses the parish offices and the St. John's Thrift Shop.
Middle: Interior of St. John Church, McLean.
In 1956, a modern church in the round was constructed.

St. Luke's "Kaffee Klatch" meets each morning after the 6:45 am Mass. Begun 30 years ago, the group provides conversation and fellowship for its members who spend a few moments after Mass before heading off to work or other activities.

Mc Lean

St. Luke

Like many other American parishes established before the 1970s, Saint Luke, founded in 1961, built a school first. Such was their conviction of the importance of Catholic education. Originally staffed by Felician sisters, today the 250-pupil award-winning school is lay staffed. The parish also sponsors a booming religious education program and a vibrant youth ministry. About forty percent of contributions in the generous parish supports education, local poor, and the world's neediest.

Saint Luke parish celebrated Mass in the gym for 20 years. In 1983, the church was dedicated. Of modern design, it was planned specifically for the celebration of

In a world of wavering standars, the traditional Blessed Sacrament Chapel is an intimate place of refuge in a steadfast parish.

the liturgy according to the directives of Vatican II. In May 1998, a new pipe organ became a source of pride. The oak instrument, surrounded by perfect acoustics, has 61 ranks and 3,169 pipes. With an emphasis on evangelization, life's sanctity, the RCIA journey and the Eucharist, 52 ministries are offered by a Lucan parish of fifteen hundred welcoming families.

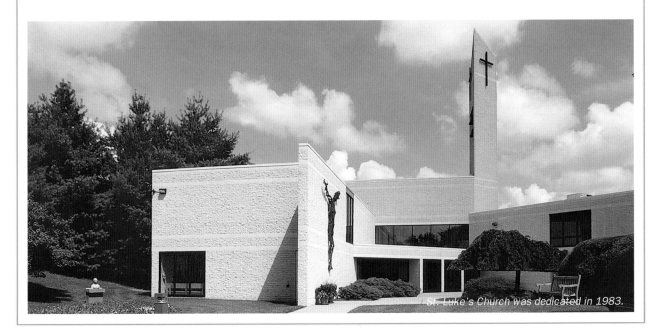

St. Luke's Church was dedicated in 1983.

MIDDLEBURG

ST. STEPHEN THE MARTYR

Founded in 1957 as a mission of St. John in Leesburg, St. Stephen the Martyr parishioners celebrated Mass in the Middleburg Community Center until the completion of the present church in 1963. Long known as a site for fox hunts, Middleburg has an aristocratic flavor, and at the time of its foundation, several of the original families wanted the new church to be called Our Lady of the Hunt.

Local legend holds that despite the relatively small number participating in the Sunday liturgy in the mission's early years, the sudden decision of the Diocese of Richmond to build a permanent church arose from the fact that the area had become the unofficial weekend residence of President John F.

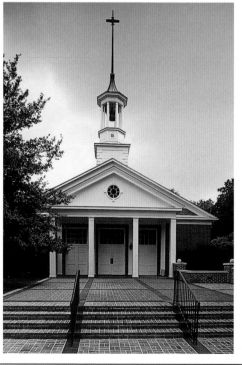

Kennedy, the first Catholic to hold the nation's highest elected office. Some old-timers claim that several members of the Secret Service helped with the construction, and at its opening, the new church included a bulletproof room in the rear for the use of the president. While it is not clear whether Kennedy ever used this specially-built space, he and his family did attend the first Mass celebrated in the new structure in April 1963. After his assassination in November of that year, a small plaque was affixed to the pew where the First Family once sat.

By 1975, the congregation of the mission church had grown sufficiently for the newly erected Diocese of Arlington to make St. Stephen an independent parish to serve southern Loudon County and the northern parts of Fauquier and Prince William Counties. Today the parish has more than 1,200 members.

Top: Built in 1963, several pews were added in the late seventies to accommodate the growing number of parishioners.
St. Stephen the Martyr, Middleburg.

St. John

Located in one of the least Catholic areas of the diocese, St. John was founded in 1946 by Missionhurst priests who staffed the parish until their withdrawal in 1995. Priests from this congregation also used to staff St. Mark in Gordonville, the only other Catholic parish in the county, but with their departure from these churches, Father David L. Martin, a priest of the Arlington diocese, was named to head both parishes.

Given the rural nature of the county, the tempo of the parish is very different from that of parishes closer to Washington, D.C. Although St. John has few formal organizations, parishioners are nevertheless involved in the life of their church and are quick to volunteer their time and talent when needed. The parish also maintains a strong religious education program. Recruiting volunteers to teach never seems to be a problem given the generosity of parishioners. Although small, the worshipping community at St. John is active.

Recently it was announced that St. Mark and St. John would be combined and formed into the new parish of St. Isidore the Farmer.

St. John, Orange. Founded in 1946 by Missionhurst priests, today the parish is served by Arlington diocesan priests.

POTOMAC FALLS

OUR LADY OF HOPE

On June 28, 2000, Bishop Loverde announced the establishment of Our Lady of Hope Parish in Potomac Falls and named Father William P. Saunders, Ph.D. as the founding pastor. With its creation Our Lady of Hope has become the sixty-sixth parish in the Arlington diocese and the sixth parish in Loudoun County, four of which have been founded since 1967.

The new parish has a twelve-acre site on which to build a church, but for the meantime, Mass is being celebrated at the Community Lutheran Church and Potomac Falls High School.

Our Lady of Hope has a twelve-acre site on which to build a church. Left to right: Philip and Sally Girardi, directors of religious education; Alexandra Bowers, parish secretary; Fr. William P. Saunders, pastor. Although the new parish lacks a permanent church, parishioners worked hard to decorate the auditorium of Potomac Falls High School for the vigil Mass of Christmas in December 2000.

PURCELLVILLE

ST. FRANCIS DE SALES

Although St. Francis de Sales Parish was not officially established until 1967, the origins of the Catholic community in Purcellville go back much farther. At the beginning of the twentieth century, Loudoun County had only one Catholic church, Immaculate Conception (now St. John's) in Leesburg. During the first

The original church was constructed in 1921

St. Francis de Sales, Purcellville.

twenty years of the century, a circuit-riding priest would celebrate Mass on a monthly basis for the Catholics of these counties, often in private homes. Eventually a mission church was built in Purcellville at Sixteenth and Main Streets and was dedicated on May 29, 1921. For some time about one hundred people would attend Sunday Mass in the small brick church with a priest traveling in from Leesburg each week.

In 1967, St. Francis de Sales was made a parish in its own right and Bishop Russell of Richmond invited the Capuchin Franciscans of the Province of the Stigmata of St. Francis to staff the newly created parish. Under the leadership of the friars, the parish continued to grow and eventually had to hold additional Sunday liturgies in leased space in Blue Ridge Middle School and later at Loudoun Valley High School.

To the chagrin of some long-time residents of Loudoun County, the 1980s brought fast and furious development to the area, and by 1990 St. Francis de Sales had more than 1,000 registered parishioners. Such growth rendered the small but quaint church in downtown Purcellville inadequate to meet the needs of the much larger congregation. Thus plans were laid for the construction of a more commodious church, which was dedicated on June 28, 1992. The new structure, built at the foot of the Blue Ridge Mountains off Route 7 and surrounded by fields, has a capacity of five hundred.

In late 1996, the provincial staff of the Capuchins announced that because of the order's declining numbers, the community could no longer provide friars to serve at St. Francis de Sales. With the departure of the friars in January 1997, Arlington diocesan priests took charge of the parish, which now has more than 3,300 parishioners.

The new church, built in 1992, can seat five hundred.

St. John Neumann, Reston.

Middle: The parish plans $6 million expansion of the church building and other facilities to start soon.
Bottom: R.C.I.A. candidates and catechumens with their sponsors and catechists after the Easter Vigil, 2001.

ST. JOHN NEUMANN

The Oblates of St. Francis de Sales have staffed St. John Neumann since its foundation in 1979. Over the years this religious congregation has been generous in its allocation of personnel to work at St. John's, and at present three Oblates on the pastoral staff minister along with a lay director of liturgical ministries. The Oblates have brought to the parish the distinctive charism of St. Francis de Sales who was known for his pioneering work in articulating a practical spirituality for lay people. The parish is proud of its association with this great saint as noted in its mission statement which calls for parishioners to "seek to reflect a gentle heart" in the living out of their Christian responsibilities.

Shortly after the construction of the first church in 1982, the parish realized that the 600-seat building would soon be too small, given the development that has continued to come to the area. After much study and discussion, plans were made to undertake a major expansion of the parish facilities starting in the spring of 2002. The church will be enlarged to accommodate a thousand worshipers, and several new classrooms will be built to serve the 1,700 children in the religious education program as well as provide space for the many activities at St. John's.

St. Thomas à Becket

Since there was no parish for Catholics living in Reston, the Reston Catholic Community, a planned community started in the late 1950s, began meeting in November 1968 as a satellite of St. Joseph Church in Herndon. By 1970 the small community had grown enough to allow Bishop John Russell of Richmond to establish St. Thomas à Becket parish. Three years later the present church was built.

St. Thomas à Becket, Reston.

At the time of the church's opening in 1973, it was the only large-sized edifice in the area suitable for religious services. For some time several other religious denominations used the space for worship, including the Northern Virginia Hebrew Congregation (NVHC). Such warm relations with persons of other faiths laid the foundation for a Catholic-Jewish dialogue, which since 1988 has sponsored an annual series of discussions between members of both congregations. In addition, NVHC uses St. Thomas for High Holy Day services, and St. Thomas uses classroom space at NVHC facilities for some of its religious education classes. St. Thomas à Becket is also an active member of Reston Interfaith, a group of churches and synagogues dedicated to the promotion of social justice in Reston.

In 1998 the parish broke ground on a new $2.5 million parish center. When completed, the new structure will contain a space for large gatherings, several meeting rooms, a commercial kitchen, offices for the religious education staff and several classrooms. The eventual opening of the center will allow the church to be used solely for worship. For lack of space, now it is used as a multi-purpose facility. In 2001, St. Thomas à Becket had more than 4,500 registered parishioners.

The present church was dedicated in 1973.

Top: At the time of its establishment as an independent parish in 1999, St. Matthew had more than two thousand parishioners. Bottom left: St. Matthew's First Holy Communion Class, 2000. Bottom right: St. Matthew, Spotsylvania.

Spotsylvania

St. Matthew

With its founding in 1999, St. Matthew became the sixty-fourth parish in the diocese of Arlington. Originally it was started as a mission of St. Patrick in Chancellorsville in 1983, but within a decade St. Matthew had more than 600 families. Its vitality prompted Bishop Loverde to make it an independent parish covering much of southern Spotsylvania County. Father David P. Meng was appointed as St. Matthew's first pastor.

ST. BERNADETTE

S t. Bernadette Parish in Springfield has experienced a seven-fold increase since its foundation, growing from 500 families in 1959 to now more than 3,500 registered families. Located in one of the fastest growing parts of Fairfax County, the parish is among the largest both in the diocese and the state. In fact, everything around the parish gives the impression of vitality and growth: the church can seat 1,500. The school has more than 500 students and the religious education program educates well over 1,000 young people. To serve so large a parish community, St. Bernadette has a large pastoral staff including four priests, two directors of religious education and a full-time youth minister.

For many years, the parish school was staffed by the Daughters of Wisdom. Because of the decline in the number of sisters, the school is now staffed by lay teachers. The remaining sisters moved to a nearby condominium and remain part of the parish community.

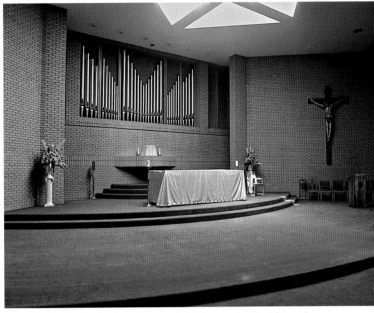

The altar in the main church was originally constructed for a Mass celebrated in 1979 by Pope John Paul II on the Mall in Washington, D.C.
Bottom: St. Bernadette Church, Springfield.

ST. WILLIAM OF YORK

Although St. William of York only became an independent parish in 1971, the origins of the Catholic community in Stafford County go back more than three centuries. The area around Aquia Harbor just north of the present church building was the site of the settlements of the first Catholic families in Virginia who came to the region around 1650. By the end of the seventeenth century, the Brents, the leading Catholic family of Virginia during colonial times, farmed several thousand acres and are buried not far from the parish in a cemetery now owned by the Arlington diocese. Despite the importance of the Brent family, the Catholic community in the area was never large, and as late as 1925 priests traveling up from Fredericksburg celebrated Mass in the homes of private families since the community was too small to maintain a regular church.

Because of the military build-up which came with World War II, in 1943 the first Catholic church building came to Stafford County with the erection of St. Therese mission church at Midway Island (near Quantico). St. Therese was established principally to serve military personnel and their families. Again, priests from St. Mary in Fredericksburg visited regularly to celebrate the sacraments, but a permanent church for the people of Stafford was to come soon. On May 8, 1956, Bishop Ireton dedicated the present St. William of York church building, yet it remained a mission of St. Mary's.

When it was finally established as a separate parish in 1971, only 25 families were officially registered. However, by the 1980s this number had increased to about 600. Because this growth included many families with young children, in 1992 the parish began operating a Catholic elementary school that

NEW CHURCH IS BEGUN—Ground is broken for a Catholic church at Aquia, to be the first ever built in Stafford County. Shovels are handled by Therese Anne Mountjoy, daughter of Mr. and Mrs. Norbert Richard Mountjoy, and the two priests who will serve the church. They are the Rev. James J. Widmer, pastor of St. Mary's Church, of Fredericksburg, in charge of the building program, and the Rev. John J. D'Connell, assistant pastor of St. Mary's. A Hampton contractor has started work with the aim of having the church ready for use by October. The brick structure, 150 feet east of U. S. Route 1 and 15 miles north of Fredericksburg, will be about 50 per cent larger than St. Mary's.

by 2001 had an enrollment of 230 students. Unlike most Catholic schools or parishes, which today have few to no religious sisters present, St. William of York was blessed with the arrival of a new group of sisters who agreed to begin a ministry in the parish. In July 1998, three Franciscan Missionary Sisters of the Infant Jesus began working in both the school and the religious education program. Their help has certainly been needed since today the parish has more than 5,100 parishioners.

Above: In 1955 ground was broken for St. William of York, the first Catholic church to be built in Stafford County. Left to right: Father James J. Widmer, Therese Anne Mountjoy and Father John J. O'Connell. Below: Interior of church.

CHRIST THE REDEEMER

Founded in 1972 to serve the Sterling Park community of eastern Loudoun County, Christ the Redeemer has been staffed by the Franciscan Friars of the Atonement since its beginning. Today the parish has more than 7,200 parishioners.

At the time of its foundation the parish held liturgies in the Sterling Middle School, but in 1979 a structure was built which included a worship space that could seat between five and seven hundred, the parish offices and a small chapel. However, even at the time of the building's opening, parish leaders knew that the structure was too small, but they were constrained by extremely high interest rates from erecting a larger, more costly building. In February 2000 finally a structure was dedicated to meet the needs of this growing parish. The new building, which includes the church, has more than 47,000 square feet of space compared with 15,000 in the old structure. In addition, 18 multi-purpose rooms are available for use by the religious education program, which has an enrollment of more than 1,000 students, as well as for other parish groups.

The new church contains a spacious sanctuary, which is visible from all parts of the building.

Since their foundation at the turn of the century, the Atonement Friars have been in the forefront in the ecumenical movement. (The community was originally started as an Anglican Franciscan foundation, but in 1909 the entire society was received into the Catholic Church.) In keeping with their special charism, the friars at Christ the Redeemer have worked over the years to build strong relations with neighboring religious congregations. In addition, the parish is involved with LINK, an organization of churches that provides material and financial assistance to the poor, a work at the heart of Franciscan spirituality.

Christ the Redeemer Parish, Sterling, dedicated a new church in February 2000.

ST. FRANCIS OF ASSISI

In 2000 the parish opened a new center to meet the needs of its growing congregation.

Realizing the need for an evangelizing missionary presence in the diocese, Bishop Ireton invited the Franciscans of Holy Name Province to staff several rural missions. The Franciscans, together with families associated with the Marine Corps base at Quantico, established St. Francis of Assisi Parish in Triangle (1957). From its beginnings as a small mission to the present 8,000 member parish, the people of St. Francis have striven to live, "as a people who know, love and serve God and the community in which they live in the Franciscan tradition of the Roman Catholic faith" (Mission Statement). The present church (1984), illuminated by classic stained glass and complemented by the sculpted figures of the Burning Bush, the Pillar of Fire, the Holy Family, the Last Supper, and the Eucharistic Sacrifice, powerfully reveals the Story of Salvation. The Parish Center (2000), concretely expresses the

Interior of St. Francis of Assisi, Triangle.

commitment to Faith Formation and Catholic Education. Francis House, the Parish Outreach Center, visibly demonstrates a desire to be, "an even greater mission oriented community than it is today" (Vision Statement).

St. Francis of Assisi, Triangle.

OUR LADY OF GOOD COUNSEL

Opening in November 1955 with 750 families, Our Lady of Good Counsel (OLGC) received Father Albert P. Campbell as its first pastor. The first Mass was held in the Dunn Loring Firehouse. Later a temporary chapel and parish center were constructed on the second floor of Frank Gadell's Food Locker.

Less than a year after its start, the new parish was given over to the care of the Oblates of St. Francis de Sales, and the parish continues to be served by men from this congregation. By 1960 a 16-classroom school and a chapel (the present-day school gym) were built. During this time OLGC also purchased the 1835 Frink house for use as a rectory. A convent was built for the Sisters of St. Joseph who staffed the parish school. In 1977 the rectory was torn down and replaced by a parish administration building, which contains residence space for the Oblates.

In 1973 the present church was built. Distinctive for the large, triangular skylight over the sanctuary, the church is used for seven Sunday liturgies, including one Spanish Mass. With more than 8,700 registered parishioners, most of the Masses are filled each Sunday. Since the parish is home to many families with children, the parish sponsors a vibrant teen ministry program, which offers both faith

The church's bell tower contains three separate bells, the largest of which weighs almost 1,500 pounds.

formation as well as opportunities for young people to socialize in a supervised setting. In addition, OLGC School (523 students) and the religious education program (300+ students) are important in the life of the parish.

Our Lady of Good Counsel Church was dedicated in 1973.

ST. MARK

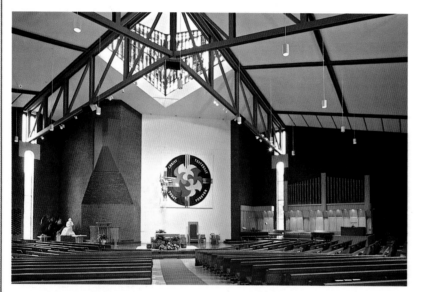

Founded in May 1965 during the Second Vatican Council, St. Mark Parish is committed to the spirit of the Council. In keeping with the Church reforms, the parish sees its support of worship, education (children and adults), youth ministry, service and community growth to be central in the life of the parish.

During St. Mark's early years, Father Robert J. Walsh, the founding pastor, put a "neighborhood group" structure into operation by which the parish was divided into small cells, each with a leader. Father Walsh would meet with the leaders on a regular basis, both to pass on information as well as get feedback on what parishioners were thinking. Popular at the time, the program has mostly died out, though a few of the groups were still in existence as recently as the early 1990s.

With a large congregation of more than 9,400 parishioners, St. Mark sponsors a myriad of groups and activities in service of the community. Some of these include: a discussion circle for returning Catholics; crisis pregnancy counseling; Tuff Times, a support group for people experiencing loss or depression; several twelve-step programs; SALT (Social Action Linking Together) and respite care to aid caregivers. In addition, St. Mark has a strong "Small Community of Faith" program. Popular in many parishes around the country, this model of faith formation brings small groups of adults together on a regular basis to foster fellowship through reflection on faith, Scripture and issues in the lives of the group's members.

Top: St. Mark Church, Vienna, was dedicated in 1984. The parish facilities include the church, chapel and parish offices.
Middle: On a sunny day, the church's many windows flood the sanctuary with light.
Bottom: Each year the pastoral council hosts a dinner for all parish volunteers. Almost 2,000 parishioners give of their time and talent to the many ministries sponsored by the parish.

ST. JOHN THE EVANGELIST

The fifth oldest parish in the diocese, St. John the Evangelist was established in 1874, although the original church was dedicated in 1861. From its opening until 1872 the new church was a mission of Sacred Heart Cathedral in Richmond, and because of the great distance between the two churches, priests could visit the mission only on an irregular basis. The parishioners decided to build a rectory in 1872, even before Father John Dougherty became the parish's first resident priest two years later. After his departure in the early 1880s, St. John fell into a period of neglect. Although Mass would be celebrated once or twice a month by circuit-riding priests, it was not until 1913 that the parish again had a resident pastor.

The postwar era brought growth to the area, and by the late 1950s it seemed that the old church was no longer adequate for the needs of St. John's growing congregation. Property was purchased on Winchester Street and even before a new church was built, in 1960 the parish erected a school. At first St. John the Evangelist School was staffed by Benedictine sisters from Bristow, but in 1968 they were replaced by the

Monument to the Sanctity of Life.

Sisters of Notre Dame (Chardon, OH). Today the 241-student school is administered by lay people.

Five years after the opening of the school, the parish dedicated the present stone church. The church is located in a residential neighborhood and provides a beautiful setting for the five liturgies that are held each weekend for its 4,500-member parish.

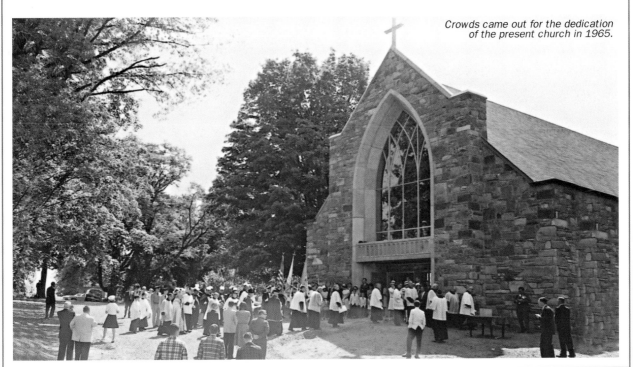

Crowds came out for the dedication of the present church in 1965.

SACRED HEART OF JESUS

In addition to being one of the westernmost parishes in the Arlington diocese, Sacred Heart of Jesus Parish is also one of the oldest churches in Northern Virginia. Although it was established as an independent parish in 1870, its real beginnings go back to 1805 with a mission chapel in Winchester. Priests came on a regular basis from Harper's Ferry to minister to the area's Catholics. The parish built a new church in 1868, which was used for more than a century until a new church was dedicated in 1989. Today Sacred Heart has almost 5,000 registered parishioners.

While the Catholic population in the area has increased tremendously since the parish's start, Sacred Heart remains the only Catholic church in Frederick County. For the past 36 years the parish has maintained a mission station in Berryville in neighboring Clarke County, one of the five counties in the diocese that does not have its own parish. When the mission was inaugurated, Mass was at first held in a movie theatre. For the past 30 years Sunday Mass has been celebrated in a local Protestant church. Some Catholics in the county attend Sunday Mass at the Trappist Holy Cross Abbey while others travel to St. Francis de Sales in Purcellville in western Loudon County. To meet the needs of the county's growing Catholic population, the parish is in the process of

Church interior.

building St. Bridget's Chapel in Berryville, which when completed, will accommodate 400.

Middle: In January 2001 students of Sacred Heart Academy gathered for a liturgy to mark "Catholic Schools Week." For many years the school was staffed by School Sisters of Notre Dame. Though the sisters are no longer present, the academy has stayed strong and today has an enrollment of 190 students.

Below: Sacred Heart, Winchester. The present church was built in 1989.

WOODBRIDGE

OUR LADY OF ANGELS

Our Lady of Angels was founded in 1958 as a mission of All Saints Parish in Manassas by priests of the Congregation of the Sacred Stigmata (Stigmatine). Only one year later Our Lady of Angels was made an independent parish. At the time of its foundation, the new parish had 230 Catholics. Today that number has grown to 40 times its original size with more than 8,000 parishioners. In 1985 a new, larger church was dedicated to meet the needs of a much larger congregation, but the 1958 brick chapel is still used for perpetual adoration of the Blessed Sacrament. In 1994 the Stigmatines withdrew from service to the parish to be replaced by diocesan priests.

Situated high above Route 1 and also close to Interstate 95, Our Lady of Angels has experienced tremendous growth in recent years, largely because of its proximity to these major thoroughfares. Residential development has been responsible for the leap in population to over 8,000 and, with the promise of continued economic expansion, there seems to be no end in sight to growth in the area. A good example of this is the ongoing increase in the number of children enrolled in the parish religious education program, which now has close to 800 students. The parish is also the site of Aquinas School, a regional Catholic elementary school serving Our Lady of Angels and parishes in Manassas and Lake Ridge. Founded in 1977 by Bishop Welsh, the school is staffed by Dominican sisters (Nashville) and lay people and has an enrollment of 540 students.

Top: Our Lady of Angels, Woodbridge.
Bottom: The original church, built in 1958, is used for perpetual adoration of the Blessed Sacrament.

St. John Bosco Parish, Woodstock, was founded in 1888.

WOODSTOCK

ST. JOHN BOSCO

Deep in the Shenandoah County, the westernmost part of the Arlington diocese, St. John Bosco Parish was founded in 1888 with the dedication of the original church. Though there was no resident pastor, priests came on a regular basis to celebrate the sacraments. During the Great Depression, the parish fell on hard times, and the church building was closed for a time. In 1940 the church was reopened with the help of visiting priests including Father Philip Weller, who traveled all the way from Washington, D.C. where he was a professor at The Catholic University of America.

In 1958 St. John Bosco received its first resident pastor when the Capuchin Franciscans, who had a seminary in Staunton, agreed to take charge of the parish. Under the leadership of the Capuchins, the parish buildings were renovated and parishioners saw a new church built. In addition, Father Salvator Ciullo, O.F.M. Cap., the first resident pastor, was able to secure the help of the Daughters of Mary, Help of Christians, a community of sisters in the tradition of Don Bosco, who both taught

catechists as well as administered a small school for grades K through three for some years.

In 1992 the parish had the misfortune to lose the services of both the Capuchin priests and the sisters. The Franciscans were replaced by Arlington diocesan priests, but no new sisters came to the parish. Small by the standards of parishes farther east, the 750-member parish remains active and supports chapters of the St. Vincent de Paul Society, the Legion of Mary and the Knights of Columbus. There is also a youth group for teens, and about 160 children are enrolled in the religious education program.

Our Lady of the Shenandoah Mission Chapel is located in Basye near the ski resort. Father Clarence M. Trinkle is often assisted at Mass by Mr. John Quinn. At 83, he is possibly the oldest altar server in the diocese.

Our Lady of Angels, Woodbridge.

Diocesan statistical information	1990	1995	2000	% Change
Catholic Population (men, women, and children)	248,876	293,664	353,367	42
Total Population (based on census estimates)	1,892,700	2,115,700	2,317,773	22
Catholics as a percentage of the total population	13 %	14 %	15 %	-
Number of Catholic households	77,341	100,929	129,249	67
Parishes	59	60	66	12
By parish, average number of parishioners	4,218	4,894	5,354	27
By parish, average number of Catholic households	1,311	1,682	1,958	49
Diocesan, active priests	94	112	130	38
Diocesan, retired priests	9	14	16	78
Catholic elementary schools	26	29	34	31
Number of elementary students	8,697	10,820	13,585	56
Diocesan Catholic high schools	3	3	3	–
Number of high school students	2,747	3,105	3,474	26
Total Catholic school teachers	548	630	1093	99
Religious education (High school)	4,137	3,006	5,122	24
Religious education (Elementary)	21,520	21,238	30,618	42
Total students under Catholic instruction	40,694	42,100	58,635	44
Infant Baptisms	5,422	5,361	7,103	31
First Communions	4,885	5,507	7,072	45
Confirmations	4,109	4,192	5,392	31

Index of Parishes

St. Timothy, Chantilly.

St. Francis of Assisi, Triangle.

Bibliography

James Henry Bailey
History of St. Peter's Church, Richmond, Virginia
(Richmond, 1959).

Gerald P. Fogarty, S.J.
Commonwealth Catholicism: A History of the Catholic Church in Virginia
(Notre Dame, IN, 2001).

James Hennesey, S.J.
American Catholics: A History of the Roman Catholic Community in the United States
(New York, 1981).

Clifford M. Lewis, S.J. and Albert J. Loomie, S.J.
The Spanish Jesuit Mission in Virginia: 1570-1572
(Chapel Hill, NC, 1953).

Francis Joseph Magri
The Catholic Church in the City and Diocese of Richmond
(Richmond, 1906).

150 Years for Christ, 1795-1945: St. Mary's Church, Alexandria
(Alexandria, 1945).

St. Mary's: 200 Years for Christ
(Alexandria, 1995).

AUTHOR
Anthony D. Andreassi

PUBLISHER
Éditions du Signe
1, rue Alfred Kastler
B.P. 94 - 67038 Strasbourg Cedex 2
France

PUBLISHING DIRECTOR
Christian Riehl

DIRECTOR OF PUBLICATIONS
Dr. Claude-Bernard Costecalde

EDITOR
Sr. Loretta Pastva, SND

PUBLISHING ASSISTANT
Joëlle Bernhard

DESIGN AND LAYOUT
Daniel Muller

PHOTOGRAPHY
Frantisek Zvardon